Richard Green Moulton, Daniel Coit Gilman, Bernard Christian
Steiner

The History of University Education in Maryland

Richard Green Moulton, Daniel Coit Gilman, Bernard Christian Steiner

The History of University Education in Maryland

ISBN/EAN: 9783337036010

Printed in Europe, USA, Canada, Australia, Japan

Cover: Foto ©ninafisch / pixelio.de

More available books at **www.hansebooks.com**

JOHNS HOPKINS UNIVERSITY STUDIES

IN

HISTORICAL AND POLITICAL SCIENCE

HERBERT B. ADAMS, Editor

History is past Politics and Politics present History—*Freeman*

NINTH SERIES

III-IV

The History of University Education in Maryland

By BERNARD C. STEINER, A. M. (Yale)

Fellow in History

The Johns Hopkins University (1876-1891)

By DANIEL C. GILMAN, LL. D.

President of the University

With Supplementary Notes on University Extension and the University of the Future, by R. G. Moulton, A. M., Cambridge, England

BALTIMORE

THE JOHNS HOPKINS PRESS

MARCH-APRIL, 1891

CONTENTS.

THE HISTORY OF UNIVERSITY EDUCATION IN MARYLAND.

By BERNARD C. STEINER.

COLONIAL ATTEMPTS TO FOUND A COLLEGE.

The State of Maryland has been almost extravagantly liberal in bestowing charters on colleges and professional schools. Over forty such charters have been given by the legislature and, in many cases, the result has proved that the gift of a charter was not warranted by the stability of the institution, to which was thus granted the power of conferring degrees. In many other cases, however, the institutions have grown and flourished, and have had an honorable history.

Collegiate education in Maryland did not begin until after the Revolution. In the colonial period there was no demand for it sufficient to warrant the establishment of a seat of higher learning. For this state of things there were several causes. The majority of the early settlers were planters and frontiersmen, having little need for an extended education and desiring it still less. Of the wealthier classes, some were like the fox-hunting English gentry, caring for little else than sport; and others, who did desire the advantages of a culture higher than that obtainable from a village schoolmaster or a private tutor, found it elsewhere. They went over to William and Mary's College in Virginia, across the ocean to England, or, in case of some Catholics like Charles Carroll, to the institutions on the continent of Europe.

7

But, though no college was established in colonial times, there was no lack of plans and attempts for one. In 1671, while as yet Harvard was the only American college, there was read and passed in the Upper House of the Assembly "An Act for the founding and Erecting of a School or College within this Province for the Education of Youth in Learning and Virtue." The Lower House amended and passed the bill; but the plan seems never to have progressed further. According to the bill the Lord Proprietor was "to Set out his Declaration of what Privileges and Immunities shall be Enjoyed by the Schollars;" and "the Tutors or School Masters" were to be of "the reformed Church of England" or, if two in number, to be "the one for the Catholick and other for the Protestants' Children."[1]

A second collegiate plan was brought before the legislature in 1732; but, having passed the Upper House, was seemingly not acted on by the Lower. This proposed college was intended to be placed at Annapolis and was to offer instruction in "theology, law, medicine, and the higher branches of a collegiate education." The governor of the colony was to be its chancellor and provision was made for a faculty of five, under whom students were to be instructed in everything from their alphabet upwards.[2]

A third unsuccessful attempt to secure the founding of a college was made in 1761,[3] and a fourth in 1763, when contrary to the earlier course of events, the rock, on which the project was shipwrecked, was found in the Upper House. The college was to be placed at Annapolis, to occupy Governor Bladen's mansion, and to have a faculty of seven masters, who were to be provided with five servants. The expense was to be defrayed from the colonial treasury, in case

---

[1] *Md. Archives;* Assembly Proceedings, 1666–1676, pp. 262–264.

[2] Scharf, *Hist. of Md.,* II, p. 510.

[3] Sharpe, *Correspondence,* Vol. II, pp. 523–5 and 545.

a tax to be levied on bachelors should prove insufficient for the purpose.[1]

The failure of these projects did not dampen the zeal of the advocates of higher education. In 1773 we find William Eddis, Surveyor of Customs at Annapolis, writing that the Legislature of the Province had determined to fit up Governor Bladen's mansion and "to endow and form a college for the education of youth in every liberal and useful branch of science," which college, "conducted under excellent regulations, will shortly preclude the necessity of crossing the Atlantic for the completion of a classical and polite education."[2] The gathering storm of war, however, drew men's attention away from this project.

THE FIRST UNIVERSITY OF MARYLAND.

The Rev. Dr. William Smith,[3] head of what is now the University of Pennsylvania, being out of employment on account of the revocation of that college's charter, was called as pastor in Chestertown on the Eastern Shore in 1780. To add to his income, he conceived the idea "of opening a school for instruction in higher branches of education." As a nucleus for his school, he took an old academy, the Kent County school, and, beginning the work of teaching, was so successful, that in 1782 the Legislature, on his application, granted the school a charter as Maryland's first college. To it the name of *Washington* was given, "in honorable and perpetual memory of His Excellency, General George Washington." Dr. Smith was so earnest and zealous in the presentation of the claims of the college, that in five years he had raised $14,000 from the people of the Eastern Shore. All seemed propitious for the college. In 1783 the first class graduated and the first degrees ever granted in Maryland were conferred, at the same time

---

[1] Scharf, *Hist. of Md.*, II, p. 511.

[2] Eddis, *Letters from Maryland*, 1769–1776.

[3] MS. sketch of Prof. Rowland Watts.

2

the corner-stone of the college building was laid, and in 1784 General Washington himself visited the college.

Dr. Smith prepared a three years' curriculum for the institution, equal to that of any college of the day and similar to the one used at the University of Pennsylvania. But the Western Shore could not endure that the educational success of its rival section of the State should so far outstrip its own. In the early days of the State, the sections were nearly equal in importance and the prevailing dualism of the political system invaded the field of education.

In 1784, two years after the founding of Washington College, *St. John's College* was chartered.[1] It was to be placed at Annapolis, and in it was merged the old county Academy, "King William's School," founded some eighty years before. By the same act, the two colleges were united in the *University of Maryland.* This University was modeled on the English type: the governor was to be its chancellor, and the governing body was to be the "Convocation of the University of Maryland." The convocation was to be composed of seven members of the Board of Visitors and Governors and two of the faculty of each college; it was to establish ordinances for the government of the colleges, to cause a uniformity in the "manners and literature," to receive appeals from the students, and to confer "the higher degrees and honors of the University." Its meetings were to be annual, and to be held alternately at each college on its commencement day.

The provisions of the act were never carried out; two fruitless attempts were made to hold sessions of Convocation in 1790 and 1791, and then nothing was even attempted. So thoroughly was the project forgotten, that the Legislature of 1805, in withdrawing the State appropriations from the two colleges, did not even mention the University, and in 1812, though the old charter had never been repealed, there was

---

[1] Act of 1784, ch. 37.

no hesitation in bestowing the name of University of Maryland on a second institution.[1]

The two colleges which constituted this first University are still existing and doing good work. The elder, Washington College, lost Dr. Smith in 1788 by his return to Philadelphia and re-accession to his old position there. He was succeeded by Rev. Colin Ferguson, a native of Kent county, and educated at Edinburgh University. Under him the college continued to flourish, until the withdrawal of the State's appropriation in 1805. The constitutionality of this withdrawal is questionable, as the original grant was to be paid annually " forever ; " but the State refused to permit itself to be sued by the college and, some years later, on increasing its appropriation to the college, the legislature required a release of all claims on the State under the original act.

By the act of 1805, the activity of the college was paralyzed and its usefulness much impaired. It had not yet become strong enough to stand alone and, when the helping hand of the State was taken away, it was almost obliged to close its doors to students. Since that time the State has renewed its grants to the college and has greatly aided it in performing its functions ; but from the disastrous effects of the act of 1805, the institution has never fully recovered.

Indeed, from 1805 to 1816, nothing but a grammar school seems to have been maintained in the college building. In the latter year, however, the college was re-opened, since the legislature had granted it a lottery of $30,000. A year later Rev. Dr. Francis Waters became " Principal," and under his able leadership the college bid fair to regain its old position ; but in 1827 a second great misfortune overtook it. On January 11, 1827, the college building was discovered to be on fire, and, in spite of the most zealous efforts, was entirely consumed. After this misfortune the college proper seems to

---

[1] Act of 1805, ch. 85. The appropriation had already been diminished by Act of 1798, ch. 107.

have been suspended a second time, and only a grammar school maintained with one instructor.   The classes were conducted in a building intended originally for a rectory, until that was destroyed by fire in 1839, when the school was again moved.

Richard W. Ringgold, the principal of the school from 1832 to 1854, seems to have been a man of ability, and under him the number of students so much increased that in 1843 it was resolved to rebuild the college on the old site and to revive the college course.   As a result, the present main building was erected, the corner-stone laid with imposing ceremonies on May 4, 1844, and the college was reopened in its own edifice on January 1, 1845.   In 1849, a class of four was graduated, and in 1854, two additional buildings were erected ; one for the Principal's residence and the other for dormitories and recitation rooms.

The college continued prosperous during the second administration of Rev. Dr. Waters from 1854 to 1860; but in the presidency of his successor, Rev. Andrew J. Sutton, came the Civil War, depriving the college of its Southern constituency and distracting men's minds from learning. After the Rebellion, an unfortunate selection of teachers and laxness of discipline caused the college to lose still more ground, and Wm. J. Rivers, Principal from 1873 to 1887, had much to do to build it up again.   He was a faithful and diligent teacher, and under him the moral tone of the college was improved and the course of instruction enlarged.   The present head, C. W. Reid, Ph. D., is still further advancing the cause of the institution and a new career of prosperity seems opening before Maryland's oldest college and the only one on the Eastern Shore of the Chesapeake Bay.

St. John's College, like its sister institution, founded on a non-denominational basis, started out under even fairer auspices.[1]   It was granted, by the State, Governor Bladen's

[1] *Centennial of St. John's.*   Address of P. R. Voorhees, Esq.

mansion and four acres of land surrounding it, was made heir
to the funds of King William's School, and secured £9,000
from private beneficence in the first two years of its history. The Bladen mansion, now known as McDowell Hall,
was repaired and enlarged and, on August 11, 1789, Bishop
Carroll was elected president of the Board of Visitors and
Governors and Dr. John McDowell accepted the Professorship of Mathematics. After unsuccessful attempts to obtain
a principal from England, Dr. McDowell was chosen to that
position in the following year and continued in office, until the
State withdrew its aid to the college in 1805. He was a man
of great learning and was very successful at St. John's and
later at the University of Pennsylvania as provost. Under
him, St. John's flourished greatly and many men of a national
reputation were enrolled among its students, from the time
the first class graduated in 1793.

The same disaster fell on St. John's, as on Washington College. The Legislature withdrew the annual grant given by
the State. The same doubt as to the constitutionality of this
withdrawal existed here, and the State confirmed its position
in the same way, by increasing its appropriation in 1832,[1] on
condition of the college's accepting it in full satisfaction of all
claims against the State under the original charter. Of late
years Maryland has been quite generous to St. John's, but it
has never quite recovered the station and prestige it lost by
the taking away of the State's grant in 1805.

In the first despair over the Act of the Legislature, the
Visitors and Governors voted to discontinue the college, but
their courage soon returned and the Rev. Bethel Judd, elected
principal in 1807, was able to graduate a class in 1810. After
his withdrawal in 1812, matters were in a disturbed state for
some years and no classes were graduated until 1822, when
Rev. Henry L. Davis, the father of Maryland's famous orator,
Henry Winter Davis, was principal. After that year there

---

[1] Resolutions of 1832, No. 41.

were no graduates until 1827, when Rev. William Rafferty
was head of the college. The struggle for existence was a
hard one and the wonder is that the college succeeded as well
as it did.

With 1831, however, began a third and more successful
period in the history of St. John's. In that year the Rev.
Hector Humphreys, then only thirty-four years of age, was
chosen president. He was a native of Connecticut and a
graduate of Yale College in 1818, and was called to St. John's
from the professorship of Ancient Languages at Washington
(Trinity) College in his native State. The effect of his energy
and devotion was soon recognized, and, largely through his
efforts, was passed the compromise of 1832. The curriculum
was enlarged, the instruction made more thorough, and classes
were yearly graduated, with but six exceptions, until his death
in 1857. His energy was very great, his learning wide and
accurate. In 1834, after travelling about the State in the
interests of the college, he succeeded in raising about $11,000,
which were used in the erection of a second building for the
college, which most appropriately has since been called by his
name. During his administration, the professors' houses were
also built, as was Pinkney Hall, a third building for the use
of the college. Dr. Humphreys also secured cabinets and
philosophical apparatus for the college and gave instruction
in Political Economy, Latin and Greek, Chemistry, Geology,
Natural Philosophy, Astronomy, Composition, Elocution,
Evidences of Christianity, Moral and Intellectual Philosophy,
Rhetoric, and Logic. Verily, an encyclopædic man of vast
industry! Only four years after Dr. Humphreys' death the
War of the Rebellion broke out, and St. John's, unlike the tem-
ple of Janus, closed its doors at the rumors of war. The
buildings were used as an hospital, and not until 1866 was
the college again reopened with the well-known educator,
Henry Barnard, at its head. In less than a year he resigned
to become the first United States Commissioner of Education,
and neither he nor his successor, Dr. James C. Welling, who

was principal until 1870, was able to graduate a class. Since the beginning of the administration of the next principal, James M. Garnett, LL. D., the succession of classes has been unbroken and the college has steadily advanced in reputation and usefulness. Dr. Garnett made the English department especially excellent and, after ten years faithful service, resigned in 1880. The Rev. J. D. Leavitt, his successor, made a departure from the old classic curriculum and organized a department of Mechanical Engineering. After he resigned Prof. W. H. Hopkins acted as principal for a time and introduced military discipline, having secured the detail of an officer from the United States Army as instructor in Military Tactics.

St. John's celebrated its centennial in 1889, and has begun its second century with excellent prospects. The four years' administration of its present principal, Thomas Fell, LL. D., has been a most successful one, and St. John's is fulfilling the purpose of its founders " to train up and perpetuate a succession of able and honest men, for discharging the various offices and duties of life, both civil and religious, with usefulness and reputation."

The Second University of Maryland.

Most universities have developed from a college; the University of Maryland differs from them, for it originated in a medical school.[1]

In 1802 Dr. John B. Davidge of Baltimore began a private class in Medicine and was so successful in it, that, in 1807, he associated with himself Drs. James Cocke and John Shaw and these three obtained from the Legislature a charter for the school, under the name of "the College of Medicine of Maryland."[2] There was made a close connection between the College of Medicine and the State " Medical and Chirurgical

---

[1] MS. Sketch of Dr. E. F. Cordell.
[2] Act of 1807, ch. 53.

Faculty," and its board of medical examiners were made
ex-officio members of the Board of Trustees of the College.
The Legislature also granted the college a lottery of $40,000.[1]

Lectures, which had been carried on at the professors' houses,
were begun in 1808, at a building on the corner of Fayette
(Chatham) street and McClellan's alley, and the first class,
consisting of five, received its degrees in 1810. As the school
grew and flourished, the ideas of its founders become more
extensive and, in 1812, a long act was passed,[2] authorizing
"the college for the promotion of medical knowledge" "to
constitute, appoint, and annex to itself the other three colleges
or faculties, viz.: The Faculty of Divinity, the Faculty of
Law, and the Faculty of the Arts and Sciences; and that the
four faculties or colleges thus united, shall be and they are
hereby constituted an university, by the name and under the
title of the University of Maryland." The connection with
the Medical and Chirurgical Faculty was severed and the
members of the four faculties, under the name of the Regents
of the University of Maryland, were to have full powers over
the University and be permitted to hold property not exceeding $100,000 in yearly value.

Each faculty was allowed to appoint its own professors and
lecturers, to choose a dean, and to exercise such powers as the
regents shall delegate. The Faculty of Physic was to be composed of the professors in the Medical College; that of Theology, of the professor of Theology and any "six ordained
ministers of any religious society or denomination;" that of
Law, of the professor of Law, "together with six qualified
members of the bar;" that of the Arts and Sciences, of the
professors in that department, "together with three of the prin-
cipals of any three academies or Colleges of the State." Such
a strangely formed and loosely united body could not succeed,
as a more homogeneous and closely compacted one would
have done.

---

[1] Act of 1807, ch. 111.   [2] Act of 1812, ch. 159.

The university was founded " on the most liberal plan, for the benefit of students of every country and every religious denomination, who shall be freely admitted to equal privileges and advantages of education, and to all the honors of the university, according to their merit, without requiring or enforcing any religious or civil test, urging their attendance upon any particular plan of religious worship or service." With these broad powers and provisions,[1] " the Faculty of Phisick, late of the College of Medicine of Maryland, * * * convened and, by the authority vested in it by said charter and with the advice and recommendations of learned men of the several professions of Divinity, Law, and the Arts and Sciences, proceeded to annex to itself the other three faculties." On April 22, 1813, the Hon. Robert Smith, formerly United States Secretary of State, was chosen the first provost, and the organization of the regents was completed.[2] A lottery of $30,000 was granted the University in 1814, and another of $100,000 in 1817.[3] From the proceeds of these lotteries and other sources was built the building of the medical department on the corner of Lombard and Greene streets. It was modelled on the Pantheon at Rome, and, when built, is said to have been without an equal in America. The medical school grew extremely fast; a loan of $30,000 from the State in 1822[4] enabled it to build a practice hall and purchase a fine collection for its museum, and the University hospital across the street was opened in 1823. In 1824 the number of students in attendance on lectures amounted to 320. The other faculties took no active steps for some time and, not until 1819, did the regents urge them to proceed to deliver lectures as soon as possible and to lay before the regents annually a report as to their progress and condition. In 1823, possibly on account

---

[1] *Records of Univ. of Md.*, Vol. A.
[2] In 1815 he was succeeded by the Rt. Rev. James Kemp, D. D.
[3] Acts of 1813, ch. 125; 1814, ch. 78.
[4] Act of 1821, ch. 88.

of this vote, Prof. David Hoffman began the instruction in
the Faculty of Law, his school being known as the " Maryland Law Institute." He published part of his lecture notes
in a book called *Legal Outlines* and continued lecturing about
ten years. After his withdrawal, the law school was given
up; but the organization of the faculty was still maintained.

The Faculty of Theology reported in 1852 " no active
organization of the faculty has ever been attempted and, in
view of the character of the department contemplated by the
charter, none seems desirable." Its only activity was a course
or two of lectures on the Evidences of Christianity, delivered
before the medical students about 1823 by the Rev. William
E. Wyatt, Professor of Theology. A nominal organization
of the faculty was kept up, however, until 1878.

The prosperity of the medical department was destroyed by
the effort of some of its professors, discontented with being
prohibited from having private classes, to have the Legislature
do away with the regents and replace them with a board of
trustees, in whom should vest the property. As early as November 12, 1824, the Regents feared trouble and obtained from
William Wirt, John Purviance and Daniel Webster, a legal
opinion that their position was inexpugnable. With this conclusion the Legislature did not agree, and on March 6, 1862,
an act was passed abolishing the Regents and appointing a
Board of twenty-one Trustees in their place.[1]

The Trustees, by decree of the courts, obtained control of the
property and forced the professors to accept them as the legal
authority. So matters went on for twelve years, until in
1837, the trustees appointed a professor personally objection-
able to some of the others, who resigned their positions under
the Trustees and opened a separate medical school in the
Indian Queen Hotel at the corner of Baltimore and Hanover
Streets. Few out-of-town students attended either school, for
the quarrel frightened them away, and the Baltimore students

[1] Act of 1825, ch. 190.

largely attended the Regents' school. Feeling ran high at one time, the Regents took possession of the University buildings by force, and bloodshed was feared.

The Board of Regents reorganized with Ashton Alexander, M. D., as Provost, and employed distinguished counsel to plead the case for them in the courts. The Legislature authorized the Court of Appeals to try the suit, and Maryland's Dartmouth College Case was decided in June, 1838, entirely in favor of the Regents. The court held that the act of 1825 was void, since it was "a judicial act, a sentence that condemned without a hearing. The Legislature has no right, without the assent of a Corporation, to alter its charter, or take from it any of its franchises or property." The Trustees would not yield at once and, in March, 1839, presented a petition to the Legislature, praying it not to pass an act requiring them to give up the property to the Regents. The memorial was referred to a joint committee, which reported a bill restoring the property to the Regents. The bill was enacted and the Regents have since ruled. During the supremacy of the Trustees, the Faculty of the Arts and Sciences was organized. They contemplated activity in 1821, and issued a circular, which drew down on them the wrath of Professor Hoffman, inasmuch as they "contemplated 'academic' instruction" not intended by the charter. The founders, he said, intended that instruction should be conveyed by lectures and that no other form of instruction should be allowed. The discussion which followed seems to show that he had the idea of having work carried on, like that done by graduate students to-day.

But nothing was done, apparently, until Baltimore College was annexed in 1830. That institution was chartered on January 7, 1804,[1] and was the development of an academy kept by James Priestley, the first president, on Paul's Lane (St. Paul Street). "It was hoped that it would, together with the other valuable seminaries of education in the same

---

[1] Act of 1803, ch. 74.

city and in the State, become adequate to the wants and wishes of our citizens," and from the proceeds of a lottery, the grant of which was an easy way for a State to be benevolent, a plain but convenient building was erected on Mulberry street.[1]

It is very doubtful if it ever graduated any students, and we learn in 1830 that "the celebrity and, in some cases, the superior existing advantages of other institutions have prevented the accomplishment of this object." Still a school had been kept up continuously, and from time to time, we catch glimpses of its lectures, &c.   In January, 1830, a joint petition of the Trustees of the University of Maryland and of Baltimore College to the Legislature "proposed the charter of Baltimore College shall be surrendered to the State, on the condition that the property belonging to the college shall be invested in the trustees of the University of Maryland."   The petition was granted,[2] and in 1832, we learn that "the Baltimore College * * * has now been merged in the University of Maryland and constitutes the chair of Ancient Languages."[3]

On October 1, 1830, the Trustees issued a prospectus, from which we learn that it was intended "to maintain an institution on the most enlarged scale of usefulness and responsibility," and that there was a "necessity for the proposed organization of a department in the University of Maryland, exclusively collegiate in its system, requiring an advanced state of classical and scientific attainments for admission to its lectures, calculated to conduct its pupils through the highest branches of a liberal education and to afford them advantages similar to what may be obtained in the distant Universities of this country and Europe." A course of study equal to that of any college of the country was announced, and a brilliant Faculty appointed; but the time was not yet come

---

[1] Scharf, *Chron. of Baltimore*, p. 294.
[2] Act of 1830, ch. 50.
[3] Lucas, *Picture of Baltimore*, p. 170.

for a great college in Baltimore and the institution languished away. In 1843, the Commissioners of Public Schools petitioned to have it transferred to the city as a High School, and in 1852, it had only one teacher and 36 scholars, a mere boys' school.

In 1854 it was reorganized as the "School of Letters under the Faculty of Arts and Sciences," with Rev. E. A. Dalrymple, formerly of the Episcopal Theological Seminary at Alexandria, as its head. On paper the course was fairly complete, and the Faculty an able one, and there were graduates in 1859, '60, '61, and '63. The course was to be a three years' one; for "the studies of Freshman year will be pursued in the preparatory department, where experience has shown they may be attended with greater advantage." Gradually students fell off, it became a mere boys' school, and finally Dr. Dalrymple was all that was left of the "School of Letters" and the "Faculty of the Arts and Sciences," and at his death, both formally became extinct.

With the restoration of the property to the Regents, the classes in the medical school increased to a size somewhat like that attained in years previous to 1825, although, owing to the opening of new schools, they never quite equalled it. During the war of the Rebellion, the school suffered from the loss of southern patronage; but at its close, students came back and the school took on fresh life. It has always been in the front rank; first of all American medical schools it recognized Gynecology as a separate branch of instruction, and it was second in making practical Anatomy a compulsory study. With the session of 1891 it will require a three years' graded course of all candidates for degrees.

In 1850 the Hon. John P. Kennedy, statesman and author, was chosen provost, and on his death in 1870, the Hon. S. Teackle Wallis was made his successor and he now fills the office with honor.

The Faculty of Law revived the Law School in the beginning of 1870, with a class of 25. An efficient faculty has caused a steady increase, until, in 1890, there were 101 students in the three years' course. The instruction is given by lectures, examinations, and moot-courts. In 1884, the Law Department moved from its former quarters in the old Baltimore College building on Mulberry Street, to a new building erected for it on the University property on Lombard Street, next to the building of the Medical Department.

In 1882, the University of Maryland obtained from the Legislature authority to open a Dental Department.[1] In 1837, the first Dental Lectures in America had been delivered before the Medical Students of the University, and it was quite fitting that there should be a dental school connected with it. The first class numbered 60, the last 132, and in eight years there have been 250 graduates. This fact and the further one that twice has it been found necessary to make large additions to the buildings of the department on Green Street, adjoining those of the Medical School, will show how rapid has been its growth.

The University has, at present, flourishing departments of Medicine, Law, and Dentistry, and worthily maintains the reputation of thorough and careful training, which it has gained in its history of eighty years.

COKESBURY COLLEGE.

In Maryland was the first Methodist Church in America, and it was natural that here too should be the first Methodist College in the world. There was no permanent organization of this denomination in the United States, until John Wesley, on the petition of the American churches, consecrated Rev. Thomas Coke, Superintendent for the United States, in 1784. Dr. Coke sailed directly from England, and arrived in New York on November 3, 1784. He thence traveled southward and, on the 15th of the same month, met Francis Asbury at

---

[1] Act of 1882, ch. 88.

Dover, Delaware. At this first meeting, Coke suggested the founding of an institution for higher education, to be under the patronage of the Methodist Church.[1] This was not a new idea to Asbury; for, four years previous to this meeting, John Dickins had made the same suggestion to him. The earlier idea had contemplated only a school, on the plan of Wesley's at Knightwood, England, and for that purpose, a subscription had been opened in North Carolina in 1781.[2]

Coke's suggestion, to have a college, was favorably received and, at the famous Christmas Conference at Baltimore in 1784, the Church was formally organized, with Coke and Asbury as Bishops, and the first Methodist College was founded. Thus the denomination which has increased to be the largest in the United States, recognized the paramount importance of education at its very foundation.[3] To the new institution, the name of Cokesbury was given, in honor of the two Bishops, from whose names the title was compounded. For this College, collections were yearly taken, amounting in 1786 to £800 and implying great self-denial by the struggling churches ill-supplied with wealth.[4]

As early as January 3, 1785, only two weeks after the College was decided on, its managers were able to report that £1,057 had been subscribed, a sum that put the enterprise on a firm footing. The site was next to be chosen, and Abingdon in Harford County was pitched upon. Of the 15,000 Methodists in the Union in 1784, over one-third were in Maryland, and hence, it had the best claim for the College, and the beauty of the situation of Abingdon charmed Coke so much that he determined upon placing the College there. It was also a place easy of access, being on the direct stage line from Baltimore to Philadelphia and near the Chesapeake Bay. Bishop Coke, the most zealous advocate of the College, contracted for the

---

[1] Stevens' *History of Methodism*, II, 253.
[2] Some account of Cokesbury. MSS. of Rev. Wm. Hamilton.
[3] *Early Schools of Methodism*, p. 21.
[4] MSS. of Rev. I. P. Cook.

building materials; but was prevented from being present at the laying of the corner-stone. Bishop Asbury, however, was present and preached a sermon on Psalms 78, verses 4 to 8.[1] In this sermon, "he dwelt on the importance of a thoroughly religious education, and looked forward to the effects, which would result to the generality, to come from the streams which should spring from this opening fountain of sanctified learning." The building was built of brick, one hundred feet in length and forty in width, faced east and west, and stood on "the summit and centre of six acres of land, with an equal proportion of ground on each side." It was said to be in architecture "fully equal, if not superior, to anything of the kind in the country." Dormitory accommodations were provided in the building; but it was intended that "as many of the students as possible, shall be lodged and boarded in the town of Abingdon among our pious friends."[2] Gardening, working in wood in a building called the "Taberna Lignaria," bathing under supervision of a master, walking, and riding were the only outdoor exercises permitted. The students were prohibited "from indulging in anything which the world calls play. Let this rule be observed with the strictest nicety; for those who play when they are young, will play when they are old."

In 1785 the Bishops issued a "Plan for Erecting a College intended to advance Religion in America." It is quite long and many of its provisions are very quaint. From it we learn that Cokesbury is intended "to receive for education and board the sons of the elders and preachers of the Methodist Episcopal Church, poor orphans, and the sons of the subscribers and other friends. It will be expected that all our friends, who send their children to the college, will, if they be able, pay a moderate sum for their education and board; the others will be taught and boarded and, if our

---

[1] Strickland's *Asbury*, p. 163.
[2] Methodist Discipline, 1789, p. 40.

finances allow it, clothed gratis. The institution is also intended for the benefit of our young men, who are called to preach, that they may receive a measure of that improvement, which is highly expedient as a preparation for public service." Teachers of ancient languages and of English will be provided, and no necessary branch of literature shall be omitted. "Above all, especial care shall be taken that due attention be paid to the religion and morals of the children, and to the exclusion of all such as continue of an ungovernable temper." "The expense of such an undertaking will be very large, and the best means we could think of, at our late conference, to accomplish our design, was to desire the assistance of all those in every place who wish well to the cause of God. The students will be instructed in English, Latin, Greek, logic, rhetoric, history, geography, natural philosophy, and astronomy. To these languages and sciences shall be added, when the finances of our college will admit of it, the Hebrew, French, and German languages. But our first object shall be, to answer the designs of *Christian* education, by forming the minds of the youth, through divine aid, to wisdom and holiness by instilling into their minds the principles of true religion—speculative, experimental, and practical—and training them in the ancient way, that they may be rational, spiritual Christians. We have consented to receive children of seven years of age, as we wish to have the opportunity of teaching 'the young idea how to shoot' and gradually forming their minds, through the divine blessing, almost from their infancy, to holiness and heavenly wisdom, as well as human learning. We shall rigidly insist on their rising early in the morning (five a. m.), and we are convinced by constant observation and experience, that it is of vast importance, both to body and mind.

"We prohibit play in the strongest terms, and in this we have the two greatest writers on the subject that, perhaps, any age has produced (Mr. Locke and Mr. Rousseau) of our sentiments; for, though the latter was essentially mistaken in his

3

religious system, yet his wisdom in other respects and extensive genius are indisputably acknowledged. The employ-
ments, therefore, which we have chosen for the recreation of
the students are such as are of greatest public utility :—agri-
culture and architecture.

"In conformity to this sentiment, one of the completest
poetic pieces of antiquity (the Georgics of Virgil) is written
on the subject of husbandry ; by the perusal of which and
submission to the above regulations, the students may delight-
fully unite the theory and practice together."

There is something extremely ludicrous in the idea of making the average student delight in spending his leisure hours
in farming, by means of a study of the Georgics in the original.
But we can hardly laugh at these men, they were too much in
earnest. To return to the circular, "The four guineas a year
for tuition, we are persuaded cannot be lowered, if we give
the students that finished education, which we are determined
they shall have. And, though our principal object is to
instruct them in the doctrines, spirit, and practice of Christianity, yet we trust that our college will, in due time, send
forth men that will be a blessing to their country in every
laudable office and employment of life, thereby uniting the
two greatest ornaments of human beings which are too often
separated : *deep learning* and *genuine piety.*"

As soon as the building was under roof, a preparatory school
was opened and the Trustees applied to John Wesley for a
President. He suggested a Rev. Mr. Heath, and this suggestion was accepted on December 23, 1786.[1] His inaugura-
tion occurred a year later and was a grand affair. Asbury
presided on each of the three days of the ceremony, and his
text on the second day, "O man of God, there is death in the
pot,"[2] was looked on by the superstitious, in time to come, as
a presage of disaster. The faculty was filled up and all seemed

[1] *Asbury's Journal,* Vol. I, p. 523.
[2] II Kings, 4: 40.

to bid fair for prosperity; but Mr. Heath remained in charge of the College less than a year, resigning because of certain charges of insufficiency, which seem rather trival. Another professor left to go into business and Asbury's soul was tried by these " heavy tidings."

The good Bishop was indefatigable in his care of Cokesbury. His visits were frequent, and while there, he was very active, examining the pupils, preaching, and arranging the affairs, both temporal and spiritual. Abingdon became a centre of Methodism, families moved there to enjoy the educational advantages, and the Conference regularly visited the College, coming over from Baltimore for that purpose.

Dr. Jacob Hall, of Abingdon, was the second President, and had under him a faculty of three professors and a chaplain. The school prospered and had public exhibitions of its students' proficiency from time to time. It is doubtful if sufficient care was exercised in the expenditure of money and, in December, 1790, the Trustees felt obliged to contract a loan of £1000. The charitable contributions fell off, and Asbury was forced to go from house to house in Baltimore, " through the snow and cold, begging money for the support of the poor orphans at Cokesbury." [1] The instruction was good, and Asbury could write to Coke, then in England, that " one promising young man has gone forth into the ministry, another is ready, and several have been under awakenings. None so healthy and orderly as our children, and some promise great talents for learning." [2] Still, " all was not well there," and on October 2, 1793, he " found matters in a poor state at college; £500 in debt, and our employes £700 in arrears." A year later, matters were desperate and the good Bishop wrote that " we now make a sudden and dead pause—we mean to incorporate and breathe and take some better plan. If we can not have a Christian school (*i. e.* a school under

---

[1] *Journal*, December 5, 1791.
[2] *Early Schools of Methodism*, p. 31.

Christian discipline and pious teachers), we will have none."[1] The project of incorporation was not favored by some, who feared that the College would not be thereby so directly under the control of the Conference, but was carried through, and the charter bears date, December 26, 1794.[2] By it, the institution was allowed to have an income not exceeding £3,000.

How a charter was to avoid increased indebtedness does not appear and the College's debt had so increased, that the Conference in 1795 decided to suspend the Collegiate Department and have only an English Free School kept in the buildings.[3]

Misfortunes never come singly: an unsuccessful attempt to burn the buildings had been made in the fall of 1788, and now, on December 4, 1795, a completely successful one was made, and the building and its contents were consumed. Rewards to discover the incendiary were offered in vain, and Asbury writes:[4] "We have a second and confirmed report that Cokesbury College is consumed to ashes—a sacrifice of £10,000 in about ten years. If any man should give me £10,000 to do and suffer again what I have done for that house, I would not do it. The Lord called not Mr. Whitefield, nor the Methodists to build colleges. I wished only for schools; Dr. Coke wanted a college. I feel distressed at the loss of the library."

Asbury despaired, but Coke did not and, going to work, he raised £1,020 from his friends. After the determination was made to move the College to Baltimore, the Church there gave £700, and a house to house solicitation brought in £600 more. A building originally erected for balls and assemblies was purchased and fitted up. It stood next the old Light Street Methodist Church and a co-educational school was opened therein on May 2, 1796. The high course planned for girls is especially noticeable at this early period. The school opened with promises of success, and within a month there were nearly 200 scholars.

[1] *Journal*, November 21, 1794.   [2] Act of 1794, ch. 21.
[3] Rev. Mr. Hamilton's MSS.   [4] *Journal*, January 5, 1796.

Fatality pursued the enterprise, however, and a year to a day from the burning of the first building, this second one was reduced to ashes, with the adjoining church and several houses.

Asbury writes rather philosophically :[1] " I conclude God loveth the people of Baltimore, and he will keep them poor to make them pure ;" but even Coke gave up hope at this new disaster, and it was twenty years before a second Methodist College was attempted.

ASBURY COLLEGE.

This was the second Methodist College in the world, and was organized in 1816, the year of Bishop Asbury's death. After a year or two of successful work, a charter was applied for and it was granted to the College February 10, 1818.[2] The President, Samuel K. Jennings, M. D., a Methodist local preacher, was a rather remarkable man. Coming from New Jersey, graduating at Rutgers, and settling in the practice of the medical profession in Virginia, he was converted by the preaching of Asbury, and was persuaded by him some years later, to move to Baltimore and take the leadership of the new enterprise.[3] He was said to be, at one time, the only Methodist preacher with a collegiate education and was well adapted to the task, from his administrative ability and wide learning. Around him, he gathered an undenominational faculty of four professors and began the life of the institution in a large brick building on the corner of Park Avenue and Franklin Street. In March, 1818, the *Methodist Magazine* tells us that there were one hundred and seventy students, and that " The Asbury College has probably exceeded in its progress, considering the short time it has been established, any literary institution in the country."[4] In that spring, a

[1] *Journal,* 1796.   [2] Act of 1817, ch. 144.
[3] Sprague, *Annals of American Pulpit,* VII, 279.
[4] *History of the M. E. Church,* Vol. III.

class was graduated, and yet only a few months later Dr. Bangs wrote that the College " continued for a short time and then, greatly to the disappointment and mortification of its friends, went down as suddenly as it had come up, and Asbury College lives only in the recollection of those who rejoiced over its rise and mourned over its fall."

This statement is not absolutely correct; it is probable that there was some catastrophe, and possibly Dr. Jennings then began to break away from the Methodist Episcopal Church, which he left entirely, when the Methodist Protestant Church was formed in 1828.   Still some sort of an organization was kept up under the old name; for does not good Hezekiah Niles, of Register fame, tell us of examinations and exhibitions he witnessed in the early spring of 1819,[1] at which time prodigies of learning and cramming were exhibited, and do we not find in 1824, a pamphlet published by Dr. Jennings, entitled " Remarks on the Subject of Education, to which are added the general rules of the school under the appellation of Asbury College." Apparently the College had passed entirely out of the control of the church, and having lowered its grade, was now little more than Dr. Jennings' private school.   The school was then situated on the corner of Charles and Baltimore Streets and, in 1833, when we catch the last glimpse of it, another removal had taken it to the corner of South and Fayette Streets.   It was then merely a boys' day school and doubtless soon perished.   So the second Methodist College failed as the first had done and another was added to the many abortive attempts to found a college in Maryland.

OTHER EXTINCT COLLEGES.

Three other attempts to found colleges demand a passing notice.

Mount Hope College stood at the corner of Eutaw Place and North Avenue, and was charted as a college in 1833.[2]

---

[1] *Niles' Register*, February 20, 1819.   [2] Act of 1832, ch. 199.

The building was constructed by the Baltimore branch of the United States Bank in 1800, during an epidemic of yellow fever in the city.   People feared to come into town to transact business and so a suburban banking house was built.   This building was bought by the Rev. Frederick Hall in 1828 and in it a school was begun, which was later expanded into the College.   The institution lasted some ten years and is worthy of note from the fact that among the teachers were two young Yale graduates, who afterwards obtained considerable renown : Professor Elias Loomis and Rev. S. W. S. Dutton.

The College of St. James was situated in Washington County and was originally intended by its founder, Bishop Whittingham, as a preparatory school.   It was opened in October, 1842, with Rev. J. B. Kerfoot,[1] afterwards Bishop of Pittsburg, as Principal, and had such speedy and encouraging success, that it was chartered as a college in 1843, under the control of the Protestant Episcopal Church.

The College prospered greatly under Bishop Kerfoot's able management, and was kept up during the War of the Rebellion in spite of the loss of Southern students, a large portion of the entire number.   In 1864, however, General Early, of the Confederate Army, invaded Maryland and took Dr. Kerfoot and Professor Coit prisoners, and the College thus forcibly discontinued, was never again reorganized.

Newton University was chartered by the Legislature[2] on March 8, 1845 and was situated on Lexington Street, between North and Calvert.   It was originally intended to combine the Baltimore preparatory schools and to furnish boys, graduating from them, the means of completing their education without leaving the city.   There was an enormous list of Trustees and the unwieldy character of the board, coupled with the irregular habits of the President, made the failure of the enterprise inevitable.   Still it offered in its catalogues

---

[1] *Life of Bishop Kerfoot*, by Rev. Hall Harrison.
[2] Act of 1844, ch. 272.

a good course of study and gave exhibitions, at which poly-
glot orations were delivered. The late Prof. Perley R. Lovejoy
was the life of the institution and, after several classes had
graduated, the University finally ceased to be, when Mr.
Lovejoy accepted a position as Professor in the Baltimore City
College.

Roman Catholic Colleges.

Maryland has been the cradle of the Roman Catholic
Church in America, as well as of the Methodist and the Pres-
byterian. The centenary of the consecration of John Carroll,
as the first Roman Catholic bishop in the United States,
occurred little more than a year ago. A few months after
Bishop Carroll's consecration, he received from the Superior
of the Order of St. Sulpice an offer to found a seminary
in Baltimore for the education of priests. This offer was
accepted and, on July 10, 1791, four Sulpician priests arrived
in Baltimore. They soon bought a house known as " One
Mile Tavern " with four acres of land and there they opened
St. Mary's Seminary, on the first Sunday in October, 1791.
The Seminary still occupies the same site, at the corner of
Paca and St. Mary's Streets. The number of the candidates
for the priesthood, who entered the Seminary, was disappoint-
ing from its smallness and, in order to procure clerics, an
Academy was opened in the rooms of the Seminary, on August
20, 1799. This was presided over by Rev. Wm. Du Bourg,
and proved so successful, as to demand a separate building.
Accordingly, the corner-stone of St. Mary's College was laid
on April 10, 1800. At Bishop Carroll's request, no American
boys were admitted for a time and only Spaniards and French
were received. In 1803, however, the College was opened to
all day scholars or boarders, without reference to birth or
religion. This step roused some opposition and many com-
munications upon the subject appeared in the newspapers,
which were afterwards collected in pamphlet form.

The students soon became numerous and the institution grew to such an extent that, in January, 1805, it was chartered as St. Mary's University. On August 13, 1806, the first class was graduated ; in that year there were 106 students. New buildings were erected and a superb botanical garden was laid out. The chapel, built soon after the incorporation, was said to be the most beautiful in the United States.

The Rev. William Du Bourg, the President, was a man of great ability and the reputation of the College rapidly spread. Many prominent men, Roman Catholics and Protestants, were graduated from St. Mary's ; but the Sulpicians felt that their vocation was to educate young men exclusively for the priesthood, and not for secular life, and they finally closed St. Mary's College in 1852, in order to devote all their energies to the Theological Seminary, which has continued its prosperous career to this present day.[1]

A second Roman Catholic College was formed by the Sulpicians in 1807 at Emmittsburg, Frederick County. It was begun by Rev. John Dubois and was soon chartered as *Mount Saint Mary's College.* The exercises were first held in a log house with a handful of pupils, who increased to 80 within five years. With the growth of the institution came the demand for larger accommodations. Better buildings were erected and a large stone edifice was undertaken in 1823. When nearly ready for occupancy, it was destroyed by fire ; but Father Dubois did not despair and, aided by the people of the vicinity, at once began a new building. In 1826 he was appointed Bishop of New York, and in the same year, the connection of the College with the Sulpician order was terminated. Although originally intended chiefly as a place for the education of clerics, Mt. St. Mary's has ever kept in view the preparation of students for a secular life, and many of its graduates have been distinguished in State, as well as in Church. In 1838, Rev. John McCaffrey, D. D., became president, and

---

[1] MSS. of Fr. G. E. Viger.

under his able control, the College prospered until 1871. During this period, the jubilee of the institution was celebrated with great ceremony in 1858. The Civil War injured the College greatly and the declaration of peace found it burdened with a heavy load of debt. For twenty years the struggle went on and it was doubtful all the time, whether the College could survive. Finally Dr. William Bryne, at his leaving the presidency in 1884, was able to report that the institution was placed on a firm financial basis as to the future, and that the debt had been reduced to $65,000. The present President, Rev. Edward P. Allen, has still further diminished the debt by more than half and the attendance has been largely increased through his efficient administration.

A third Roman Catholic College is *St. Charles's*, situated in Howard County, near Ellicott City. It is situated on land given by Charles Carroll of Carrollton, and was chartered on February 3, 1830,[1] its name being taken from that of its founder and of the great Archbishop of Milan.[2] The institution was placed under the control of the Society of St. Sulpice and was established " exclusively for the education of pious young men of the Catholic persuasion for the ministry of the Gospel." The corner-stone was laid by the venerable Charles Carroll, on July 11, 1831 ; but, for want of funds to carry on the work successfully, the institution was not opened until the fall of 1848. The first President, Rev. O. L. Jenkins, began the institution with four pupils, and at his death in 1869, the number had grown to 140. Since the closing of St. Mary's College in 1852, St. Charles's has been used by the Sulpicians as preparatory to St. Mary's Seminary.

To supply the want of a college, to which Baltimore boys of Roman Catholic families could go without leaving home, *Loyola College* was opened in September, 1852. It is under the control of the Jesuits and has confined itself to receiving day scholars.

---

[1] Act of 1830, ch. 50.　　[2] MSS. of Rev. G. E. Viger.

The fifth and last Roman Catholic College, **Rock Hill,** was chartered in 1865.[1] It is situated near Ellicott City, as is St. Charles's, and is under the supervision of the Brothers of the Christian Schools. It prepares youth for the various duties and occupations of life with great thoroughness, and has ever been noted especially for the attention paid to the development of the body as well as the mind of its pupils.

WESTERN MARYLAND COLLEGE.

In 1865, Mr. Fayette R. Buell began an academy for boys and girls at Westminster, Carroll County,[2] and, in the spring of 1866, he proposed to the Conference of the Methodist Protestant Church, of which he was a member, that the school should be chartered as a college and taken under the Church's patronage. This proposition was not acceded to, but Mr. Buell went on with his plan. Confidence in the Rev. J. T. Ward, one of the teachers in Mr. Buell's school, induced two of his friends to lend the enterprise $10,000, and the corner-stone of the College building was laid on September 6, 1886. The College opened a year later with seventy-three pupils. In February, 1868, Mr. Buell found himself so much in debt, that he appealed to the Conference to take the property off his hands. This was done, and a Board of Trustees appointed by the Conference was incorporated by the legislature on March 30, 1868.

The next fall, the institution reopened with Rev. J. T. Ward as President, in which office he continued for seventeen years. These were years of trouble and severe work to make the College a success. There was no endowment, and only by the most strenuous efforts was the College saved on several occasions from being overwhelmed with debt. Still, in spite of all disadvantages, good work was done and valuable experience was gained. The College has been a co-educational one

[1] Act of 1865, ch. 10.   [2] Lewis, *Outline of Western Maryland College.*

from the first, and connected with it was a department of Biblical Literature, for such as intended to become clergymen, until a separate Theological School was opened in 1882. During Dr. Ward's administration, new buildings were erected and, at his resignation in 1886, he left the institution ready to be made still more efficient by his successor. Rev. Thomas H. Lewis succeeded as President and, while he has caused the work and equipment of the College to be further enlarged, he has also been successful in paying off the last dollar of the debt that had hung over it so long as an incubus.   .

FEMALE EDUCATION.

The Baltimore Female College, so long presided over by Dr. N. C. Brooks, was the pioneer institution in Maryland for the higher education of women. Founded in 1849, it long had a prosperous existence; but finally was obliged to close its doors in June, 1890, on account of the withdrawal of the grant formerly given by the State.

Besides this institution there was no successful attempt in Maryland to found a college for female education, until the *Woman's College of Baltimore* was chartered in 1884.[1] It was founded by the Methodist Episcopal Church, in honor of the centenary of its organized existence in this country, and is "denominational but not sectarian." For it beautiful buildings, adjoining the First Methodist Church, have been erected on St. Paul Street. Much of the money for its endowment was given by the present President, the Rev. J. F. Goucher, D. D., and, largely through his influence, was it able to open its doors to students on September 13, 1888. It has determined, very sensibly, to grant no degrees, save to those thoroughly fitted to receive them, and so has had no graduates up to the present. Its growth under the care of W. H. Hopkins, Ph. D., its first President, was great in numbers and

---

[1] MSS. of Pres. W. H. Hopkins.

endowment and the prospects are now fair for this Baltimore Woman's College taking high rank among similar institutions.

CONCLUSION.

To a superficial observer from a distance, it sometimes seems as if University education in Maryland began with the foundation of the Johns Hopkins University, a sketch of which follows from the pen of its honored President. Our study into the history of education in the State, however, has shown us that Maryland, instead of being one of the latest of the United States to conceive the University idea, was, in fact, one of the very earliest, and that her institutions have a history of which they need not be ashamed; though their work has not been so widely known as some others and though the bright promise of morning, in many cases, has not been followed by the full development of noontide.

The patient labors of William Smith, of Hector Humphreys, of Francis Asbury, of John Dubois, and of many others, have been far from lost. Wherein they failed, they gained valuable experience for their successors, and wherein they succeeded, they helped to instil "into the minds and hearts of the citizens, the principles of science and good morals."

THE JOHNS HOPKINS UNIVERSITY

(1876-1891).

BY DANIEL C. GILMAN.

FOUNDATION.

The year 1876 is commonly taken as the date of the foundation of the Johns Hopkins University, as in that year its doors were opened for the reception of students. On the twenty-second of February the plans of the University were publicly made known, and consequently " Washington's Birthday " has since been observed as an anniversary or commemoration day. But in reality the Trustees were organized nine years before. The founder, Johns Hopkins, as he saw the end of life approaching (although he continued in active business for several years afterwards), determined to bestow a large part of his fortune upon two institutions which he proposed to establish, a University and a Hospital. These establishments were to be managed by separate Boards of Trustees, citizens of Baltimore, whom he selected for their integrity, wisdom, and public spirit. In order that the two Boards might be closely allied, the founder was careful that a majority of the Trustees of one corporation should also be a majority of the Trustees of the other corporation, and in a letter which he left as the final expression of his wishes, he declared it to be his " constant wish and purpose that the Hospital should ultimately

39

form a part of the Medical School of the University." The Hospital was opened for the reception of patients in May, 1889; and a volume which was prepared in the following year by Dr. J. S. Billings, gives a full description of the buildings, with other papers illustrative of the history and purposes of that great charity. But as the Medical School, which is to form the bond of union between the two establishments has not yet been organized, the following statements will only refer to those opportunities which are here provided for the study of science and literature, in the faculty commonly known as the faculty of philosophy and the liberal arts.

Before speaking of his gifts, a few words should be devoted to the memory of Johns Hopkins. This large-minded man, whose name is now renowned in the annals of American philanthropy, acquired his fortune by slow and sagacious methods. He was born in Anne Arundel county, Maryland, not far from the city of Annapolis, of a family which for several generations had adhered to the views of the Society of Friends. His ancestors were among the earliest settlers of the colony. While still a boy, Johns Hopkins came to Baltimore without any capital but good health, the good habits in which he had been brought up, and unusual capacity for a life of industrious enterprise. He began on the lowest round of the ladder of fortune, and by his economy, fidelity, sagacity, and perseverance he rose to independence and influence. He was called to many positions of financial responsibility, among the most important being that of President of the Merchants' National Bank, and that of a Director in the Baltimore and Ohio Railroad Company. He was a man of positive opinions in political affairs, yet he never entered political life; and although he contributed to the support of educational and benevolent societies he was not active in their management. In the latter part of his life, he dwelt during the winter in a large mansion, still standing on the north side of Saratoga street, west of North Charles street, and during the

summer on an estate called Clifton, in Baltimore County.
In both these places he exercised hospitality without osten-
tation. He bought a large library and many oil paintings
which are now preserved in a memorial room at the Hospital. Nevertheless, his pursuits were wholly mercantile, and
his time and strength were chiefly devoted to the business in
which he was engaged,—first as a wholesale grocer, and afterwards as a capitalist interested in many and diverse financial
undertakings. More than once, in time of commercial panic,
he lent his credit to the support of individuals and firms with
a liberality which entitled him to general gratitude. He died
in Baltimore, December 24, 1873, at the age of seventy-nine
years. He had never married. After providing for his near
relations, he gave the principal part of his estate to the two
institutions which bear his name, the Johns Hopkins University and the Johns Hopkins Hospital. Each of them received
property estimated in round numbers at three and a half
million dollars. The gift to the University included his
estate of Clifton (three hundred and thirty acres of land),
fifteen thousand shares of the common stock of the Baltimore
and Ohio Railroad, and other securities which were valued at
seven hundred and fifty thousand dollars.

Many persons have expressed surprise that Mr. Hopkins
should have made so large an investment in one corporation.
But the stock of the Baltimore and Ohio Railroad was free from
taxation, for many years it paid a dividend of ten per cent.
per annum, and the managers, of whom he was one, con-
fidently anticipated that a large stock dividend would be
declared at an early day. Mr. Hopkins not only gave to the
University all the common stock that he held in this corporation ;
he also advised that the Trustees should not dispose of it, nor
of the stock accruing thereon by way of increment or dividend.
In view of the vibrations to which this stock was subjected
during the fifteen years subsequent to the death of Mr. Hopkins, it should not be forgotten that it was his will that
linked the fortune of the great educational institution, which

4

he founded, to the fortune of another corporation, in which
he had the highest confidence. Fortunately, the crisis into
which this union led, has been successfully passed. The
friends of the University generously subscribed for its support an "emergency fund" of more than $100,000. Other
large gifts were made and others still are known to be in the
future. The Trustees, moreover, have changed four-fifths of
their holdings of the common stock of the railroad company
above mentioned, into its preferred stock, from which a
permanent income of six per centum will be derived. The
finances of the University are now on a solid basis, although
additional gifts will be required for the construction of buildings and for the enlargement of the course of study, and
still more before a medical department can be instituted.

Preliminary Organization.

The Johns Hopkins University was incorporated under the
laws of the State of Maryland, August 24, 1867. Three
years later, June 13, 1870, the Trustees met and elected a
President and a Secretary of the Board. They did not meet
again until after the death of Mr. Hopkins, when they
entered with a definite purpose on the work for which they
were associated. They collected a small but excellent library
of books, illustrating the history of the universities of this
and of other lands; they visited in a body Cambridge, New
Haven, Ithaca, Ann Arbor, Philadelphia, Charlottesville,
and other seats of learning; they were favored with innu-
merable suggestions and recommendations from those who
knew much about education, and from those who knew
little; and they invited several scholars of distinction to
give them their counsel. Three presidents of colleges gave
them great assistance, answering in the frankest manner
all the searching questions which were put to them by a
sagacious committee. Grateful acknowledgments will always
be due to these three gentlemen: Charles W. Eliot, LL. D.,

President of Harvard University, Andrew D. White, LL. D., President of Cornell University, and James B. Angell, LL. D., President of the University of Michigan.

INAUGURAL ASSEMBLY.

The election of a President of the University took place in December, 1874. He entered upon the duties of his station in the following spring, and in the summer of 1875, at the request of the Trustees, he went to Europe and conferred with many leaders of university education in Great Britain and on the continent. At the same time he visited many of the most important seats of learning. During the following winter the plans of the University were formulated and were made public in the Inaugural Address of the President, which was delivered on the 22nd of February, 1876, before a large audience assembled in the Academy of Music.

On this occasion, the Governor of the State, Hon. John Lee Carroll; the Mayor of the City, Hon. Ferdinand C. Latrobe; the Presidents and representative Professors of a large number of Universities and Colleges; the Trustees and other officers of the scientific, literary and educational institutions of Baltimore; the State and City officers of public instruction and other invited guests, together with the Trustees of Johns Hopkins, occupied the platform. The house was filled with an attentive audience.

At eleven o'clock, the chair was taken by the President of the Trustees, Mr. Galloway Cheston. The orchestra of the Peabody Institute, directed by Professor Asger Hamerik, performed several pieces of classical music.

A prayer was then offered up by Rev. Alfred M. Randolph, D. D., of Emmanuel Church, now Assistant Bishop of Virginia, after which the Chairman of the Executive Committee, Mr. Reverdy Johnson, Jr., said:

"Our gathering to-day is one of no ordinary interest. From all sections of our State, from varied sections of our

land, we have met at the opening of another avenue to social
progress and national renown.   After two years of pressing
responsibility and anxious care the Trustees of the Johns
Hopkins University present the first detailed account of
their trust.   Of the difficulties attending the discharge of
their duty ; of the nice balancing of judgment ; of the careful
investigation and continued labor called for in the organization
of the University, this is not the place to speak ; but for the
Board of Trustees, I may be allowed to claim the credit of
entire devotion to the work, and a sincere desire to make of
the University all that the public could expect from the
generous foundation.   Happily, our action is unfettered, and
where mistakes occur, as occur they must, the will and power
are at hand to correct them.   We may say that the University's birth takes place today, and I do not think it mere
sentiment, should we dwell with interest upon its concurrence
with the centennial year of our national birth, and the birthday of him who led the nation from the throes of battle to
maturity and peace.   But it is not my province to detain you
from the exercises which are to follow.   I am happy to state
that we have among us to-day one who represents the highest
type of American education, and one who, from the beginning,
has sympathized with, counselled and aided us.   I know you
anticipate me, as I announce the distinguished name, from the
most distinguished seat of learning in our land—President
Eliot, of Harvard University."

ADDRESS OF PRESIDENT ELIOT.

President Eliot next delivered a Congratulatory Address
in which he said :
"The oldest University of the country cordially greets the
youngest, and welcomes a worthy ally—an ally strong in
material resources and in high purpose.
"I congratulate you, gentlemen, Trustees of the Johns
Hopkins University, upon the noble work which is before

you. A great property, an important part of the fruit of a long life devoted with energy and sagacity to the accumulation of riches, has been placed in your hands, upon conditions as magnanimous as they are wise, to be used for the public benefit in providing for coming generations the precious means of liberal culture. Your Board has great powers. It must hold and manage the property of the University, make all appointments, fix all salaries, and, while leaving both legislative and administrative details to the several faculties which it will create, it must also prescribe the general laws of the University. Your cares and labor will grow heavy as time goes on; but in accordance with an admirable usage, fortunately established in this country, you will serve without other compensation than the public consideration which will justly attach to your office, and the happy sense of being useful. The actuating spirit of your Board will be a spirit of scrupulous fidelity to every trust reposed in you, and of untiring zeal in promoting the welfare of the University and the advancement of learning. Judged by its disinterestedness, its beneficence and its permanence, your function is as pure and high as any that the world knows, or in all time has known. May the work which you do in the discharge of your sacred trust be regarded with sympathetic and expectant forbearance by the present generation, and with admiration and gratitude by posterity.

" The University which is to take its rise in the splendid benefaction of Johns Hopkins must be unsectarian. None other could as appropriately be established in the city named for the Catholic founder of a colony to which all Christian sects were welcomed, or in the State in which religious toleration was expressly declared in the name of the Government for the first time in the history of the Christian world. There is a too common opinion that a college or university which is not denominational must therefore be irreligious; but the absence of sectarian control should not be confounded with lack of piety. A university whose officers and students are divided among many sects need no more be irreverent and irreligious than the community which in respect to diversity of creeds it resembles.   It would be a fearful portent if thorough study of nature and of man in all his attributes and works, such as befits a university, led scholars to impiety. But it does not; on the contrary, such study fills men with humility and awe, by bringing them on every hand face to face with inscrutable mystery and infinite power.   The whole work of a university is uplifting, refining and spiritualizing: it embraces

> whatsoever touches life
> With upward impulse; be He nowhere else,
> God is in all that liberates and lifts;
> In all that humbles, sweetens and consoles.

"A university cannot be built upon a sect, unless, indeed, it be a sect which includes the whole of the educated portion of the nation.   This University will not demand of its officers and students the creed, or press upon them the doctrine of any particular religious organization; but none the less—I should better say, all the more—it can exert through high-minded teachers a strong moral and religious influence.   It can implant in the young breasts of its students exalted sentiments and a worthy ambition; it can infuse into their hearts the sense of honor, of duty, and of responsibility.

"I congratulate the city of Baltimore, Mr. Mayor, that in a few generations she will be the seat of a rich and powerful university.   To her citizens its grounds and buildings will in time become objects of interest and pride.   The libraries and other collections of a university are storehouses of the knowledge already acquired by mankind, from which further invention and improvement proceed.   They are great possessions for any intelligent community.   The tone of society will be sensibly affected by the presence of a considerable number of highly educated men, whose quiet and simple lives are devoted to philosophy and teaching, to the exclusion of the common objects of human pursuit.   The University will hold high the standards of public duty and public spirit, and will enlarge that cultivated class which is distinguished, not by wealth merely, but by refinement and spirituality.

"I felicitate the State of Maryland, whose Chief Magistrate honors this assembly with his presence, upon the establishment within her borders of an independent institution of the highest education. The elementary school is not more necessary to the existence of a free State than the University. The public school system depends upon the institutions of higher education, and could not be maintained in real efficiency without them. The function of colleges, universities, and professional schools is largely a public function; their work is done primarily, indeed, upon individuals, but ultimately for the public good. They help powerfully to form and mould aright the public character; and that public character is the foundation of everything which is precious in the State, including even its material prosperity. In training men thoroughly for the learned professions of law and medicine, this University will be of great service to Maryland and the neighboring States. During the past forty years the rules which governed admission to these honorable and confidential professions have been carelessly relaxed in most of the States of the Union, and we are now suffering great losses and injuries, both material and moral, in consequence of thus thoughtlessly abandoning the safer ways of our fathers. It is for the strong universities of the country to provide adequate means of training young men well for the learned professions, and to set a high standard for professional degrees.

"President Gilman, this distinguished assembly has come together to give you God-speed. I welcome you to arduous duties and grave responsibilities. In the natural course of life you will not see any large part of the real fruits of your labors; for to build a university needs not years only, but generations; but though 'deeds unfinished will weigh on the doer,' and anxieties will sometimes oppress you, great privileges are nevertheless attached to your office. It is a precious privilege that in your ordinary work you will have to do only with men of refinement and honor; it is a glad and animating sight to see successive ranks of young men pressing year by year into the battle of life, full of hope and courage, and each year better armed and equipped for the strife; it is a privilege to serve society and the country by increasing the means of culture; but, above all, you will have the great happiness of devoting yourself for life to a noble public work without reserve, or stint, or thought of self, looking for no advancement, 'hoping for nothing again.' Knowing well by experience the nature of the charge which you this day publicly assume, familiar with its cares and labors, its hopes and fears, its trials and its triumphs, I give you joy of the work to which you are called, and welcome you to a service which will task your every power.

" The true greatness of States lies not in territory, revenue, population, commerce, crops or manufactures, but in immaterial or spiritual things; in the purity, fortitude and uprightness of their people, in the poetry, literature, science and art which they give birth to, in the moral worth of their history and life. With nations, as with individuals, none but moral supremacy is immutable and forever beneficent. Universities, wisely directed, store up the intellectual capital of the race, and become fountains of spiritual and moral power. Therefore our whole country may well rejoice with you, that you are auspiciously founding here a worthy seat of learning and piety. Here may young feet, shunning the sordid paths of low desire and worldly ambition, walk humbly in the steps of the illustrious dead—the poets, artists, philosophers and statesmen of the past; here may fresh minds explore new fields and increase the sum of knowledge; here from time to time may great men be trained up to be leaders of the people; here may the irradiating light of genius sometimes flash out to rejoice mankind; above all, here may many generations of manly youth learn righteousness."

INAUGURAL ADDRESS OF THE FIRST PRESIDENT.

In his inaugural address, the President of the Johns Hopkins University, after a grateful reference to the founder and his generosity, and a reminder that the endowment, large as it appears, is not large when compared with the acquisitions of many other institutions, called attention to some of the special distinctions of this gift. Among them were named : the freedom from conditions ; the absence of political or ecclesiastical control ; the connection with an endowed hospital ; the geographical advantages of Baltimore ; and the timeliness of the foundation. Five agencies for the promotion of superior instruction were next briefly discussed, universities, learned academies, colleges, technical schools, and museums. The object of these paragraphs was to suggest the distinctive Idea of the University, and to show that while forms and methods vary in different countries, the freedom for investigation, the obligation to teach, and the careful bestowal of academic honors are always understood to be among the university functions. Wherever a strong university is established, learned societies, colleges, technical schools, and museums are clustered. It is the sun and they are the planets.

Twelve points were then enumerated on which there is a consensus so general that further discussion seemed needless.

1. All sciences are worthy of promotion ; or in other words, it is useless to dispute whether literature or science should receive most attention, or whether there is any essential difference between the old and the new education.

2. Religion has nothing to fear from science, and science need not be afraid of religion. Religion claims to interpret the word of God, and science to reveal the laws of God. The interpreters may blunder, but truths are immutable, eternal, and never in conflict.

3. Remote utility is quite as worthy to be thought of as immediate advantage. Those ventures are not always most sagacious that expect a return on the morrow. It sometimes

pays to send our argosies across the seas,—to make investments with an eye to slow but sure returns. So it is always
in the promotion of science.

4. As it is impossible for any university to encourage with
equal freedom all branches of learning, a selection must be
made by enlightened governors, and that selection must
depend on the requirements and deficiencies of a given people, in a given period. There is no absolute standard of
preference. What is more important at one time or in one
place may be less needed elsewhere and otherwise.

5. Individual students cannot pursue all branches of learning, and must be allowed to select, under the guidance of
those who are appointed to counsel them. Nor can able
professors be governed by routine. Teachers and pupils must
be allowed great freedom in their method of work. Recitations, lectures, examinations, laboratories, libraries, field exercises, travel, are all legitimate means of culture.

6. The best scholars will almost invariably be those who
make special attainments on the foundation of a broad and
liberal culture.

7. The best teachers are usually those who are free, com-
petent, and willing to make original researches in the library
and the laboratory.

8. The best investigators are usually those who have also
the responsibilities of instruction, gaining thus the incitement
of colleagues, the encouragement of pupils, the observation of
the public.

9. Universities should bestow their honors with a sparing
hand; their benefits most freely.

10. A university cannot be created in a day; it is a slow
growth. The University of Berlin has been quoted as a proof
of the contrary. That was indeed a quick success, but in an
old, compact country, crowded with learned men eager to
assemble at the Prussian court. It was a change of base
rather than a sudden development.

11. The object of the university is to develop character—to make men. It misses its aim if it produces learned pedants, or simple artisans, or cunning sophists, or pretentious practitioners. Its purport is not so much to impart knowledge to the pupils, as to whet the appetite, exhibit methods, develop powers, strengthen judgment, and invigorate the intellectual and moral forces. It should prepare for the service of society a class of students who will be wise, thoughtful, progressive guides in whatever department of work or thought they may be engaged.

12. Universities easily fall into ruts. Almost every epoch requires a fresh start.

If these twelve points are conceded, our task is simplified, though it is still difficult. It is to apply these principles to Baltimore in 1876. We are trying to do this with no controversy as to the relative importance of letters and science, the conflicts of religion and science, or the relation of abstractions and utilities; our simple aim is to make scholars, strong, bright, useful and true.

Proceeding to speak of the Johns Hopkins University, the speaker then announced that at first the Faculty of Philosophy would alone be organized, where instruction would be given in language, mathematics, ethics, history and science. The Medical Faculty would not long be delayed. That of Jurisprudence would come in time. That of Theology is not now proposed.

The next paragraphs of the address will be given without abbreviation.

Who shall our teachers be?

This question the public has answered for us; for I believe there is scarcely a preëminent man of science or letters, at home or abroad, who has not received a popular nomination for the vacant professorships. Some of these candidates we shall certainly secure, and their names will be one by one made known. But I must tell you, in domestic confidence, that it is not an easy task to transplant a tree which is deeply

rooted.   It is especially hard to do so in our soil and climate.
Though a migratory people, our college professors are fixtures.
Such local college attachments are not known in Germany;
and the promotions which are frequent in Germany are less
thought of here.   When we think of calling foreign teachers,
we encounter other difficulties.   Many are reluctant to cross
the sea; and others are, by reason of their lack of acquaintance
with our language and ways, unavailable.   Besides we may
as well admit that London, Paris, Leipsic, Berlin, and Vienna
afford facilities for literary and scientific growth and influence,
far beyond what our country affords.   Hence, it is probable
that among our own countrymen, our faculty will be chiefly
found.

I wrote, not long ago, to an eminent physicist, presenting
this problem in social mechanics, for which I asked his solu-
tion.   "We cannot have a great university without great
professors; we cannot get great professors till we have a
great university: help us from the dilemma."   Let me tell
his answer: "Your difficulty," he says, "applies only to
old men who are great; these you can rarely move; but the
young men of genius, talent, learning and promise, you can
draw.   They should be your strength."

The young Americans of talent and promise—there is our
strength, and a noble company they are!   We do not ask from
what college, or what state, or what church they come; but
what do they know, and what can they do, and what do they
want to find out.

In the biographies of eminent scholars, it is curious to
observe how many indicated in youth preëminent ability.
Isaac Casaubon, whose name in the sixteenth century shed
lustre on the learned circles of Geneva, Montpellier, Paris,
London and Oxford, began as professor of Greek, at the age
of twenty-two; and Heinsius, his Leyden contemporary, at
eighteen.   It was at the age of twenty-eight, that Linnaeus
first published his *Systema Naturæ.*   Cuvier was appointed a
professor in Paris at twenty-six, and, a few months later, a

member of the Institute. James Kent, the great commentator on American law, began his lectures in Columbia College at the age of thirty-one. Henry was not far from thirty years of age when he made his world-renowned researches in electro-magnetism; and Dana's great work on mineralogy was first published before he was twenty-five years old, and about four years after he graduated at New Haven. Look at the Harvard lists :—Everett was appointed Professor of Greek at twenty-one; Benjamin Peirce, of Mathematics at twenty-four; and Agassiz was not yet forty when he came to this country. For fifty years Yale College rested on three men selected in their youth by Dr. Dwight, and almost simultaneously set at work; Day was twenty-eight, Silliman, twenty-three, and Kingsley, twenty-seven, when they began their professorial lives. The University of Virginia, early in its history, attracted foreign teachers, who were all young men.

We shall hope to secure a strong staff of young men, appointing them because they have twenty years before them, selecting them on evidence of their ability; increasing constantly their emoluments, and promoting them because of their merit to successive posts, as scholars, fellows, assistants, adjuncts, professors and university professors. This plan will give us an opportunity to introduce some of the features of the English fellowship and the German system of privat-docents; or in other words, to furnish positions where young men desirous of a university career may have a chance to begin, sure at least of a support while waiting for promotion.

Our plans begin but do not end here. As men of distinction, who have won the highest rank in their callings, are known to be free, we shall invite them to come among us.

If we would maintain a university, great freedom must be allowed both to teachers and scholars. This involves freedom of methods to be employed by the instructors on the one hand, and on the other, freedom of courses to be selected by the students.

But this freedom is based on laws,—two of which canno be too distinctly or too often enunciated. A law which shoul govern the admission of pupils is this, that before they wi this privilege they must have been matured by the long preparatory discipline of superior teachers, and by the sys tematic, laborious, and persistent pursuit of fundamenta knowledge; and a second law, which should govern the worl of professors, is this, that with unselfish devotion to the dis covery and advancement of truth and righteousness, they renounce all other preferment, so that, like the greatest of al teachers, they may promote the good of mankind.

I see no advantage in our attempting to maintain the tra ditional four-year class-system of the American colleges. I has never existed in the University of Virginia; it is modified though not nominally given up at Harvard; it is not a important characteristic of Michigan and Cornell; it is no known in the English, French or German universities. It i a collegiate rather than a university method. If parents o students desire us to mark out prescribed courses, eithe classical or scientific, lasting four years, it will be easy to d so. But I apprehend that many students will come to u excellent in some branches of a liberal education and deficien in others—good perhaps in Greek, Latin and mathematics deficient in chemistry, physics, zoölogy, history, politica economy, and other progressive sciences. I would give t such candidates on examination, credit for their attainments and assign them in each study the place for which they ar fitted. A proficient in Plato may be a tyro in Euclid. Moreover, I would make attainments rather than time the condition of promotion; and I would encourage every schola to go forward rapidly or go forward slowly, according to the fleetness of his foot and his freedom from impediment. In other words, I would have our University seek the good of individuals rather than of classes.

The sphere of a university is sometimes restricted by its walls or is limited to those who are enrolled on its lists.

There are three particulars in which we shall aim at extra-mural influence: first, as an examining body, ready to examine and confer degrees or other academic honors on those who are trained elsewhere; next, as a teaching body, by opening to educated persons (whether enrolled as students or not) such lectures as they may wish to attend, under certain restrictions —on the plan of the lectures in the high seminaries of Paris; and, finally, as in some degree at least a publishing body, by encouraging professors and lecturers to give to the world in print the results of their researches.

What are we aiming at?

An enduring foundation; a slow development; first local, then regional, then national influence; the most liberal pro-motion of all useful knowledge; the special provision of such departments as are elsewhere neglected in the country; a generous affiliation with all other institutions, avoiding inter-ferences, and engaging in no rivalry; the encouragement of research; the promotion of young men; and the advance-ment of individual scholars, who by their excellence will advance the sciences they pursue, and the society where they dwell.

No words could indicate our aim more fitly than those by which John Henry Newman expresses his "Idea of the Uni-versity," in a page glowing with enthusiasm, to which I delight to revert.

What will be our agencies?

A large staff of teachers; abundance of instruments, appa-ratus, diagrams, books, and other means of research and instruction; good laboratories, with all the requisite facilities; accessory influences, coming both from Baltimore and Wash-ington; funds so unrestricted, charter so free, schemes so elastic, that as the world goes forward, our plans will be adjusted to its new requirements.

What will be our methods?

Liberal advanced instruction for those who want it; dis-tinctive honors for those who win them; appointed courses for those who need them; special courses for those who can take no other; a combination of lectures, recitations, laboratory practice, field work and private instruction; the largest discretion allowed to the Faculty consistent with the purposes in view; and, finally, an appeal to the community to increase our means, to strengthen our hands, to supplement our deficiencies, and especially to surround our scholars with those social, domestic and religious influences which a corporation can at best imperfectly provide, but which may be abundantly enjoyed in the homes, the churches and the private associations of an enlightened Christian city.

Citizens of Baltimore and Maryland.—This great undertaking does not rest upon the Trustees alone; the whole community has a share in it. However strong our purposes, they will be modified, inevitably, by the opinions of enlightened men; so let parents and teachers incite the youth of this commonwealth to high aspirations; let wise and judicious counsellors continue their helpful suggestions, sure of being heard with grateful consideration; let skilful writers, avoiding captiousness on the one hand and compliment on the other, uphold or refute or amend the tenets here announced; let the guardians of the press diffuse widely a knowledge of the benefits which are here provided; let men of means largely increase the usefulness of this work by their timely gifts.

At the moment there is nothing which seems to me so important, in this region, and indeed in the entire land, as the promotion of good secondary schools, preparatory to the universities. There are old foundations in Maryland which require to be made strong, and there is room for newer enterprises, of various forms. Every large town should have an efficient academy or high school; and men of wealth can do no greater service to the public than by liberally encouraging, in their various places of abode, the advanced instruction of the young. None can estimate too highly the good which came to England from the endowment of Lawrence Sheriff at Rugby, and of Queen Elizabeth's school at Westminster, or the value to New England of the Phillips foundations in Exeter and Andover.

Every contribution made by others to this new University will enable the Trustees to administer with greater liberality their present funds. Special foundations may be affiliated with our trust, for the encouragement of particular branches of knowledge, for the reward of merit, for the construction of buildings; and each gift, like the new recruits of an army, will be more efficient because of the place it takes in an organized and efficient company. It is a great satisfaction in this world of changes and pecuniary loss to remember what safe investments have been made at Harvard and Yale, and other old colleges, where dollar for dollar is still shown for every gift.

The atmosphere of Maryland seems favorable to such deeds of piety, hospitality and " good-will to men." George Calvert, the first Lord Baltimore, comes here, returns to England and draws up a charter which becomes memorable in the annals of civil and religious liberty, for which, " he deserves to be ranked," (as Bancroft says), " among the most wise and benevolent lawgivers of all ages;" among the liberals of 1776 none was bolder than Charles Carroll of Carrollton ; John Eager Howard, the hero of Cowpens, is almost equally worthy of gratitude for the liberality of his public gifts ; John McDonogh, of Baltimore birth, bestows his fortune upon two cities for the instruction of their youth ; George Peabody, resident here in early life, comes back in old age to endow an Athenæum, and begins that outpouring of munificence which gives him a noble rank among modern philanthropists; Moses Sheppard bequeaths more than half a million for the relief of mental disease ; Rinehart, the teamster boy, attains distinction as a sculptor, and bequeaths his hard-won acquisitions for the encouragement of art in the city of his residence ; and a Baltimorean still living, provides for the foundation of an astronomical observatory in Yale College ; while Johns Hopkins lays a foundation for learning and charity, which we celebrate to-day.

5

The closing sentences of the discourse were addressed to the young men of Baltimore and to the Trustees.

THE FACULTY.

One of the earliest duties which devolved upon the President and Trustees, after deciding upon the general scope of the University, was to select a staff of teachers by whose assistance and counsel the details of the plan should be worked out. It would hardly be right in this place to recall the distinctive merits of the able and learned scholars who have formed the academic staff during the first fourteen years, but perhaps the writer may be allowed to pay in passing a tribute of gratitude and respect to those who entered the service of the University at its beginning. To their suggestions, their enthusiasm, their learning, and above all their freedom from selfish aims and from petty jealousies, must be attributed in a great degree the early distinction of this institution. They came from widely distant places; they had been trained by widely different methods; they had widely different intellectual aptitudes; but their diversities were unified by their devotion to the university in which they were enlisted, and by their desire to promote its excellence. This spirit has continued till the present time, and has descended to those who have from time to time joined the ranks, so that it may be emphatically said that the union of the Faculty has been the key to its influence.

The first requisite of success in any institution is a staff of eminent teachers, each of whom gives freely the best of which he is capable. The best varies with the individual; one may be an admirable lecturer or teacher; another a profound thinker; a third a keen investigator; another a skilful experimenter; the next, a man of great acquisitions; one may excel by his industry, another by his enthusiasm, another by his learning, another by his genius; but every member of a faculty should be distinguished by some uncommon attainments and by some special aptitudes, while the faculty as a whole should be united and coöperative. Each professor, according to his subject and his talents, should have his own best mode of working, adjusted to and controlled by the exigencies of the institution with which he is associated.

The original professors, who were present when instructions began in October, 1876, were these: as the head and guide of the mathematical studies, Professor Sylvester, of Cambridge, Woolwich and London, one of the foremost of European mathematicians; as the leader of classical studies, Professor Gildersleeve, then of the University of Virginia; as director of the Chemical Laboratory and of instruction in chemistry, Professor Remsen, then of Williams College; to organize the work in Biology (a department then scarcely known in American institutions, but here regarded as of great importance with reference to the future school of medicine), Professor Martin, then of Cambridge (Eng.), a pupil of Professor Michael Foster and of Professor Huxley; as chief in the department of Physics, Professor Rowland, then holding a subordinate position in the Rensselaer Polytechnic Institute, whose ability in this department had been shown by the contributions he had made to scientific journals; and as collegiate professor, or guide to the undergraduate students, Professor Charles D. Morris, once an Oxford fellow, and then of the University of the City of New York.

The names of the professors in the Faculty of Philosophy, from 1876 to 1890, are as follows, arranged in the order of their appointment:

1876......BASIL L. GILDERSLEEVE, LL. D.....*Greek.*
1876......J. J. SYLVESTER, LL. D..............*Mathematics.*
1876......IRA REMSEN, Ph. D....................*Chemistry.*
1876......HENRY A. ROWLAND, Ph. D.........*Physics.*
1876......H. NEWELL MARTIN, Sc. D..........*Biology.*
1876......CHARLES D. MORRIS, A. M............*Classics, (Collegiate).*
1883......PAUL HAUPT, Ph. D...................*Semitic Languages.*
1884......G. STANLEY HALL, LL. D............*Psychology.*
1884......WILLIAM H. WELCH, M. D...........*Pathology.*
1884......SIMON NEWCOMB, LL. D..............*Mathematics and Astronomy.*

1886......John H. Wright, A. M...............*Classical Philology.*
1889......Edward H. Griffin, LL. D........*History of Philosophy.*
1891......Herbert B. Adams, Ph. D...........*Amer. and Inst. History.*
1891......William K. Brooks, Ph. D.........*Animal Morphology.*

The persons below named have been appointed associate professors,—and their names are arranged in the order of their appointment :

1883......Herbert B. Adams, Ph. D............*History.*
1883......Maurice Bloomfield, Ph. D........*Sanskrit and Comp. Philology.*
1883......William K. Brooks, Ph. D..........*Animal Morphology.*
1883......Thomas Craig, Ph. D.................*Mathematics.*
1883.....Charles S. Hastings, Ph. D........*Physics.*
1883......Harmon N. Morse, Ph. D... ....*Chemistry.*
1883......William E. Story, Ph. D............*Mathematics.*
1883..... Minton Warren, Ph. D..............*Latin.*
1884......A. Marshall Elliot, Ph. D........*Romance Languages.*
1884......J. Rendel Harris, A. M............*New Testament Greek.* ·
1885......George H. Emmott, A. M...........*Logic.*
1885......C. René Gregory, Ph. D..............*New Testament Greek.*
1885......George H. Williams, Ph. D........*Inorganic Geology.*
1885......Henry Wood, Ph. D................... *German.*
1887......Richard T. Ely, Ph. D...............*Political Economy.*
1888......William T. Councilman, M. D.... *Anatomy.*
1888......William H. Howell, Ph. D........*Animal Physiology.*
1888......Arthur L. Kimball, Ph. D.........*Physics.*
1888......Edward H. Spieker, Ph. D.........*Greek and Latin.*
1889......Louis Duncan, Ph. D...................*Electricity.*
1889......Fabian Franklin, Ph. D............*Mathematics.*

At the opening of the Johns Hopkins Hospital, the principal physicians and surgeons of that foundation were appointed professors of the University, namely, arranged in the order of their appointment :

1889......William Osler, M. D............. ...*Medicine.*
1889......Henry M. Hurd, M. D...............*Psychiatry.*
1889......Howard A. Kelly, M. D............*Gynecology.*
1889......William S. Halsted, M. D.........*Surgery.*

In selecting a staff of teachers, the Trustees have endeavored to consider especially the devotion of the candidate to some particular line of study and the certainty of his eminence in that specialty ; the power to pursue independent and original investigation, and to inspire the young with enthusiasm for study and research ; the willingness to coöperate in building up a new institution; and the freedom from tendencies toward ecclesiastical or sectional controversies. They announced that they would not be governed by denominational or geographical considerations in the appointment of any teacher ; but would endeavor to select the best person whose services they could secure in the position to be filled,—irrespective of the place where he was born, or the college in which he was trained, or the religious body with which he might be enrolled.

It is obvious that in addition to the qualifications above mentioned, regard has always been paid to those personal characteristics which cannot be rigorously defined, but which cannot be overlooked if the ethical as well as the intellectual character of a professorial station is considered, and if the social relations of a teacher to his colleagues, his pupils, and their friends, are to be harmoniously maintained. The professor in a university teaches as much by his example as by his precepts.

Besides the resident professors, it has been the policy of the University to enlist from time to time the services of distinguished scholars as lecturers on those subjects to which their studies have been particularly directed. During the first few years the number of such lecturers was larger, and the duration of their visits was longer than it has been recently. When the faculty was small, the need of the occasional lecturer was more apparent for obvious reasons, than it has been in later days. Still the University continues to invite the coöperation of non-resident professors, and the proximity of Baltimore to Washington makes it particularly easy to engage learned gentlemen from the capital to give occasional lectures upon their favorite studies. Recently a lectureship of Poetry has

been founded by Mr. and Mrs. Turnbull of Baltimore, in
memory of a son who is no longer living, and an annual
course may be expected from writers of distinction who are
known either as poets, or as critics, or as historians of poetry.
The first lecturer on this foundation will be Mr. E. C.
Stedman, of New York, the second, Professor Jebb, of
Cambridge (Eng.).   Another lectureship has been instituted
by Mr. Eugene Levering with the object of promoting the
purposes of the Young Men's Christian Association.   The
first lecturer on this foundation was Rev. Dr. Broadus, of
Louisville, Ky.

A few of those who held the position of lecturers made
Baltimore their home for such prolonged periods that they
could not properly be called non-resident.   The following
list contains the principal appointments.   It might be much
enlarged by naming those persons who have lectured at the
request of one department of the University and not of the
Trustees, and by naming some who gave but single lectures.

1876......Simon Newcomb..........................*Astronomy.*
1876......Léonce Rabillon........................*French.*
1877......John S. Billings......................*Medical History, etc.*
1877......Francis J. Child......................*English Literature.*
1877......Thomas M. Cooley......................*Law.*
1877......Julius E. Hilgard ....*Geodetic Surveys.*
1877......James Russell Lowell..............*Romance Literature.*
1877......John W. Mallet.........................*Technological Chemistry.*
1877......Francis A. Walker.....................*Political Economy.*
1877......William D. Whitney..................*Comparative Philology.*
1878......William F. Allen......................*History.*
1878......William James.........................*Psychology.*
1878......George S. Morris......................*History of Philosophy.*
1879......J. Lewis Diman........................*History.*
1879......H. Von Holst..........................*History.*
1879......William G. Farlow..................*Botany.*
1879......J. Willard Gibbs......................*Theoretical Mechanics.*
1879......Sidney Lanier.........................*English Literature.*
1879......Charles S. Peirce.....................*Logic.*
1880......John Trowbridge.......................*Physics.*
1881......A. Graham Bell........................*Phonology.*

1881......S. P. LANGLEY.............................*Physics.*
1881......JOHN MCCRADY...........................*Biology.*
1881......JAMES BRYCE..............................*Political Science.*
1881......EDWARD A. FREEMAN..................*History.*
1881......JOHN J. KNOX.............................*Banking.*
1882......ARTHUR CAYLEY...........................*Mathematics.*
1882......WILLIAM W. GOODWIN..................*Plato.*
1882......G. STANLEY HALL........................*Psychology.*
1882......RICHARD M. VENABLE..................*Constitutional Law.*
1882......JAMES A. HARRISON.....................*Anglo-Saxon.*
1882......J. RENDEL HARRIS.....................*New Testament Greek.*
1883......GEORGE W. CABLE.......................*English Literature.*
1883......WILLIAM W. STORY.....................*Michel Angelo.*
1883......HIRAM CORSON............................*English Literature.*
1883......F. SEYMOUR HADEN.....................*Etchers and Etching.*
1883......JOHN S. BILLINGS........................*Municipal Hygiene.*
1883......JAMES BRYCE..............................*Roman Law.*
1883......H. VON HOLST.............................*Political Science.*
1884......WILLIAM TRELEASE.....................*Botany.*
1884......J. THACHER CLARKE....................*Explorations in Assos.*
1884......JOSIAH ROYCE.............................*Philosophy.*
1884......WILLIAM J. STILLMAN..................*Archæology.*
1884......CHARLES WALDSTEIN....................*Archæology.*
1884......SIR WILLIAM THOMSON................*Molecular Dynamics.*
1885......A. MELVILLE BELL.....................*Phonetics, etc.*
1885......EDMUND GOSSE...........................*English Literature.*
1885......EUGENE SCHUYLER......................*U. S. Diplomacy.*
1885......JUSTIN WINSOR...........................*Shakespeare.*
1885......FREDERICK WEDMORE.................*Modern Art.*
1886......ISAAC H. HALL...........................*New Testament.*
1886......WILLIAM HAYES WARD................*Assyria.*
1886......WILLIAM LIBBEY, JR...................*Alaska.*
1886......ALFRED R. WALLACE...................*Island Life.*
1886......MANDELL CREIGHTON...................*Rise of European Universities.*
1887......ARTHUR L. FROTHINGHAM, JR........*Babylonian and Assyrian Art.*
1887......RODOLFO LANCIANI.....................*Roman Archæology.*
1888......ANDREW D. WHITE......................*The French Revolution.*
1890......JOHN A. BROADUS.......................*Origin of Christianity.*

The number of associates, readers, and assistants has been very large, most such appointments having been made for brief periods among young men of promise looking forward to preferment in this institution or elsewhere.

Distinction between Collegiate and University Courses.

From the opening of the University until now a sharp distinction has been made between the methods of university instruction and those of collegiate instruction. In the third annual report, September 1, 1878, the views which had been announced at the opening of the University are expanded and are illustrated by the action of the Trustees and the Faculty during the first two years.

The terms university and college have been so frequently interchanged in this country that their significance is liable to be confounded; and it may be worth while, once more at least, to call attention to the distinction which is recognized among us. By the college is understood a place for the orderly training of youth in those elements of learning which should underlie all liberal and professional culture. The ordinary conclusion of a college course is the Bachelor's degree. Usually, but not necessarily, the college provides for the ecclesiastical and religious as well as the intellectual training of its scholars. Its scheme admits but little choice. Frequent daily drill in languages, mathematics, and science, with compulsory attendance and frequent formal examinations, is the discipline to which each student is submitted. This work is simple, methodical, and comparatively inexpensive. It is understood and appreciated in every part of this country.

In the university more advanced and special instruction is given to those who have already received a college training or its equivalent, and who now desire to concentrate their attention upon special departments of learning and research. Libraries, laboratories, and apparatus require to be liberally provided and maintained. The holders of professorial chairs must be expected and encouraged to advance by positive researches the sciences to which they are devoted; and arrangements must be made in some way to publish and bring before the criticism of the world the results of such investigations. Primarily, instruction is the duty of the professor in a uni-

versity as it is in a college; but university students should
be so mature and so well trained as to exact from their
teachers the most advanced instruction, and even to quicken
and inspire by their appreciative responses the new investigations which their professors undertake. Such work is costly
and complex; it varies with time, place, and teacher; it is
always somewhat remote from popular sympathy, and liable
to be depreciated by the ignorant and thoughtless. But it is
by the influence of universities, with their comprehensive
libraries, their costly instruments, their stimulating associations and helpful criticisms, and especially their great professors, indifferent to popular applause, superior to authoritative
dicta, devoted to the discovery and revelation of truth, that
knowledge has been promoted, and society released from the
fetters of superstition and the trammels of ignorance, ever
since the revival of letters.

In further exposition of these views, from men of different
pursuits, reference should be made to an article on Classics
and Colleges, by Professor Gildersleeve (*Princeton Review*,
July, 1878), lately reprinted in the author's "Essays and
Studies," (Baltimore, 1890); to an address by Professor
Sylvester before the University on "Mathematical Studies
and University Life," (February 22, 1877); to an address by
Professor Martin on the study of Biology (*Popular Science
Monthly*, January, 1877); to some remarks on the study of
Chemistry by Professor Remsen (*Popular Science Monthly*,
April, 1877); and to an address entitled "A Plea for Pure
Science" (Salem, 1883), by Professor Rowland, as a Vice-
President of the American Association for the Advancement
of Science. Although of a much later date, reference should
also be made to an address by Professor Adams (February
22, 1889) on the work of the Johns Hopkins University,
printed in the *Johns Hopkins University Circulars*, No. 71.
An address by Dr. James Carey Thomas, one of the Trustees,
at the tenth anniversary, in 1886, may also be consulted
(*Ibid.* No. 50). Reference may also be made to the fifteen
annual reports of the University and to the articles below

named, by the writer of this sketch.   The Group System of
College Courses in the Johns Hopkins University (*Andover
Review*, June, 1886); The Benefits which Society derives
from Universities : Annual Address on Commemoration Day,
1885 (*Johns Hopkins University Circulars*, No. 37); article on
Universities in Lalor's *Cyclopædia of Political Science ;* an
address before the Phi Beta Kappa Society of Harvard University, July 1, 1886 ; an address at the opening of Bryn
Mawr College, 1885.

STUDENTS, COURSES OF STUDIES, AND DEGREES.

In accordance with the plans thus formulated, the students
have included those who have already taken an academic
degree, and who have here engaged in advanced studies;
those who have entered as candidates for the Bachelors'
degree ; and those who have pursued special courses without
reference to degrees.   The whole number of persons enrolled
in these three classes during the first fourteen years (1876–
1890) is fifteen hundred and seventy-one.   Seven hundred
and three persons have pursued undergraduate courses and
nine hundred and two have followed graduate studies.   Many
of those who entered as undergraduates have continued as
graduates, and have proceeded to the degree of Doctor of
Philosophy.   These students have come from nearly every
State in the Union, and not a few of them have come from
foreign lands.   Many of those who received degrees before
coming here were graduates of the principal institutions of
this country.   The degree of Doctor of Philosophy has been
awarded after three years or more of graduate studies to one
hundred and eighty-four persons, and that of Bachelor of Arts
to two hundred and fifty at the end of their collegiate course.

Two degrees, and two only, have been opened to the students
of this University.   Believing that the manifold forms in which
the baccalaurate degree is conferred are confusing the public,
and that they tend to lessen the respect for academic titles, the
authorities of the Johns Hopkins University determined to

bestow upon all those who complete their collegiate courses the title of Bachelor of Arts. This degree is intended to indicate that its possessor has received a liberal education, or in other words that he has completed a prolonged and systematic course of studies in which languages, mathematics, sciences, history, and philosophy have been included. The amount of time devoted to each of these various subjects varies according to individual needs and preference, but all the combinations are supposed to be equally difficult and honorable. Seven such combinations or groups of studies have been definitely arranged, and "the group system," thus introduced, combines many of the advantages of the elective system, with many of the advantages of a fixed curriculum. The undergraduate has his choice among many different lines of study, but having made this determination he is expected to follow the sequence prescribed for him by his teachers. He may follow the old classical course ; or he may give decided preference to mathematics and physics; or he may select a group of studies, antecedent to the studies of a medical school ; or he may pursue a scientific course in which chemistry predominates ; or he may lay a foundation for the profession of law by the study of history and political science ; or he may give to modern languages the preference accorded in the first group to the ancient classics. In making his selection, and indeed in prosecuting the career of an undergraduate, he has the counsel of some member of the faculty who is called his adviser. While each course has its predominant studies, each comprises in addition the study of French and German, and at least one branch of science, usually chemistry or physics, with laboratory exercises.

The degree of Doctor of Philosophy is offered to those who continue their studies in a university for three years or more after having attained the baccalaureate degree. Their attention must be given to studies which are included in the faculty of philosophy and the liberal arts, and not to the professional faculties of Law, Medicine, and Theology. Students who have graduated in other institutions of repute may offer

themselves as candidates for this degree. In addition to the
requirements above mentioned, the student must show his
proficiency in one principal subject and in two that are
secondary, and must submit himself to rigid examinations,
first written and then oral. He must also present a thesis
which must gain the approval of the special committee to
which it may be referred, and must subsequently be printed.
All these requisitions are enforced by a faculty which is known
as the Board of University Studies.

As an encouragement to the systematic prosecution of university studies, the degree of Doctor of Philosophy in this
University is offered under the following conditions.

A Board of University Studies is constituted for the purpose of guiding the work of those who may become candidates
for this degree. The time of study is a period of at least
three years of distinctive university work in the philosophical
Faculty. It is desirable that the student accepted as a candidate should reside here continuously until his final examinations are passed, and he is required to spend the last year
before he is graduated in definite courses of study at this University. Before he can be accepted as a candidate, he must
satisfy the examiners that he has received a good collegiate
education, that he has a reading knowledge of French and
German, and that he has a good command of literary expression. He must also name his principal subject of study and
the two subordinate subjects.

The Board reserves the right to say in each case whether
the antecedent training has been satisfactory, and, if any of
the years of advanced work have been passed by the candidate
away from this University, whether they may be regarded
as spent in university studies under suitable guidance and
favorable conditions. Such studies must have been pursued
without serious distractions and under qualified teachers.

Private study, or study pursued at a distance from libraries
and laboratories and other facilities, will not be considered as
equivalent to university study.

In the conditions which are stated below, it will appear that there are several tests of the proficiency of the candidate, in addition to the constant observation of his instructors. A carefully prepared thesis must be presented by the candidate on a subject approved by his chief adviser, and this thesis must receive the approbation of the Board. There are private examinations of the candidate, both in his chief subject and in the subordinate subjects. If these tests are successfully passed, there is a final oral examination in the presence of the Board.

As an indication of the possible combinations which may be made by those who are studying for the degree of Doctor of Philosophy, the following schedule is presented :

Physics, Mathematics, and Chemistry; Animal Physiology, Animal Morphology, and Chemistry; Chemistry, Mineralogy, and Geology; Mathematics, Astronomy, and Physics; Sanskrit, Greek, and Latin; History, Political Economy, and International Law; Greek, Sanskrit, and Latin; French, Italian and Spanish, and German; Latin, Sanskrit, and Roman Law; Latin, Sanskrit, and German; Assyriology, Ethiopic and Arabic, and Greek; Political Economy, History, and Administration; English, German, and Old Norse; Inorganic Geology and Petrography, Mineralogy, and Chemistry; Geology and Mineralogy, Chemistry, and Physics; Romance Languages, German, and English; Latin, Greek, and Sanskrit; German, English, and Sanskrit.

While students are encouraged to proceed to academic degrees, the authorities have always borne in mind the needs of those who could not, for one reason or another, remain in the university for more than a year or two, and who might wish to prosecute their studies in a particular direction without any reference to academic honors. Such students have always been welcome, especially those who have been mature enough to know their own requirements and to follow their chosen courses, without the incentive of examinations and diplomas.

PUBLICATIONS, SEMINARIES, SOCIETIES.

The Johns Hopkins University has encouraged publication. In addition to the annual Register or Catalogue, the report of the President is annually published, and from time to time during the year "Circulars" are printed, in which the progress of investigations, the proceedings of societies, reports of lectures, and the appearance of books and essays are recorded. Encouragement is also given by the Trustees to the publication of literary and scientific periodicals and occasionally of learned essays and books. The journals regularly issued are :

I. *American Journal of Mathematics.* S. Newcomb, Editor, and T. Craig, Associate Editor. Quarterly. 4to. Volume XIII in progress.

II. *American Chemical Journal.* I. Remsen, Editor. 8 nos. yearly. 8vo. Volume XIII in progress.

III. *American Journal of Philology.* B. L. Gildersleeve, Editor. Quarterly. 8vo. Volume XI in progress.

IV. *Studies from the Biological Laboratory.* H. N. Martin, Editor, and W. K. Brooks, Associate Editor. 8vo. Volume V in progress.

V. *Studies in Historical and Political Science.* H. B. Adams, Editor. Monthly. 8vo. Vol. IX in progress.

VI. *Contributions to Assyriology, etc.* Fr. Delitzsch and Paul Haupt, Editors. Vol. II in progress.

VII. *Johns Hopkins University Circulars.* 85 numbers issued.

Another form of intellectual activity is shown in the seminaries and scientific associations which have more or less of an official character. In the seminary, the professor engages with a small company of advanced students, in some line of investigation—the results of which, if found important, are often published. The relations of the head of a seminary to those whom he admits to this advanced work, are very close. The younger men have an opportunity of seeing the methods by which older men work. The sources of knowledge, the so-called authorities, are constantly examined. The drift of modern discussions is followed. Investigations, sometimes of a very special character, are carefully prosecuted. All this is done upon a plan, and with the incessant supervision of the director, upon whose learning, enthusiasm, and suggestiveness, the success of the seminary depends. Each such seminary among us has its own collection of books.

The associations or societies serve a different purpose. They bring together larger companies of professors and graduate students, who hear and discuss such papers as the members may present. These papers are not connected by one thread like those which come before the seminaries. They are usually of more general interest, and they often present the results of long continued thought and investigation.

BUILDINGS, LIBRARIES, AND COLLECTIONS.

The site selected when the University was opened in the heart of Baltimore, near the corner of Howard and Monument streets, has proved so convenient, that from time to time additional property in that neighborhood has been secured and the buildings thus purchased have either been modified so as to meet the academic needs, or have given place to new and commodious edifices.

The principal buildings now in use are these:

(1). A central administration building, in which are the class-rooms for classical and oriental studies.

(2). A library building, in which are also rooms devoted especially to history and political science.

(3). A chemical laboratory well equipped for the service of more than a hundred workers.

(4). A biological laboratory, with excellent arrangements for physiological and morphological investigations.

(5). A physical laboratory—the latest and best of the laboratories—with excellent accommodations for physical research and instruction.

(6). A gymnasium for bodily exercise.

(7). Two dwelling houses, appropriated to the collections in mineralogy and geology until a suitable museum and laboratory can be constructed.

(8). Levering Hall, constructed for the uses of the Young Men's Christian Association, and containing a large hall which may be used for general purposes.

(9). Smaller buildings used for the smaller classes.

(10). An official residence of the President, which came to the University as a part of the bequest of the late John W. McCoy, Esq.

The library of the university numbers nearly 45,000 well selected volumes,—including "the McCoy library" not yet incorporated with the other books, and numbering 8,000 volumes. Not far from 1,000 periodicals are received, from every part of the civilized world. Quite near to the university is the Library of the Peabody Institute, a large, well-chosen, well-arranged, and well-catalogued collection. It numbers more than one hundred thousand volumes.

The university has extensive collections of minerals and fossils, a select zoölogical and botanical museum, a valuable collection of ancient coins, a remarkable collection of Egyptian antiquities (formed by Col. Mendes I. Cohen, of Baltimore), a bureau of maps and charts, a number of noteworthy autographs and literary manuscripts of modern date, and a large amount of the latest and best scientific apparatus—astronomical, physical, chemical, biological, photographical, and petrographical.

STATISTICS.

Summary of Attendance, 1876–90.

Years.	Teachers.	Total Enrolled Students.	Graduates.	Matriculates.	Special.	Degrees Conferred.	
						A. B.	Ph. D.
1876–77......	29	89	54	12	23	—	—
1877–78......	34	104	58	24	22	—	4
1878–79......	25	123	63	25	35	3	6
1879–80......	33	159	79	32	48	16	5
1880–81......	39	176	102	37	37	12	9
1881–82......	43	175	99	45	31	15	9
1882–83......	41	204	125	49	30	10	6
1883–84......	49	249	159	53	37	23	15
1884–85......	52	290	174	69	47	9	13
1885–86......	49	314	184	96	34	31	17
1886–87......	51	378	228	108	42	24	20
1887–88......	57	420	231	127	62	34	27
1888–89......	55	394	216	129	49	36	20
1889–90......	58	404	229	130	45	37	33
1890–91......	64	427	231	142	54	—	—

TRUSTEES.

It should never be forgotten in considering the history of such a foundation that the ultimate responsibility for its organization and government rests upon the Board of Trustees. If they are enlightened and high-minded men, devoted to the advancement of education, their influence will be felt in every department of instruction. The Johns Hopkins University has been exceptionally favored in this respect. Mr. Hopkins chose the original body with the same sagacity that he showed in all his career as a business man; and as, one by one, vacancies have occurred, men of the same type have been selected, by coöptation, for these important positions. The names of the Trustees from the beginning are as follows:

*1867	GEORGE WILLIAM BROWN.
*1867	GALLOWAY CHESTON.
1867	GEORGE W. DOBBIN.
*1867	JOHN FONERDEN.
*1867	JOHN W. GARRETT.
1867	CHARLES J. M. GWINN.
1867	LEWIS N. HOPKINS.
*1867	WILLIAM HOPKINS.
1867	REVERDY JOHNSON, JR.
1867	FRANCIS T. KING.
*1867	THOMAS M. SMITH.
1867	FRANCIS WHITE.
1870	JAMES CAREY THOMAS.
1878	C. MORTON STEWART.
1881	JOSEPH P. ELLIOTT.
1881	J. HALL PLEASANTS.
1881	ALAN P. SMITH.
1886	ROBERT GARRETT.
1891	JAMES L. McLANE.

* Deceased.

Notes supplementary to the Johns Hopkins University
Studies in Historical and Political Science, 1891, No. 1.

UNIVERSITY EXTENSION AND THE UNIVERSITY OF THE FUTURE.

THE SUBSTANCE OF ADDRESSES DELIVERED BEFORE THE JOHNS HOPKINS AND OTHER UNIVERSITY AUDIENCES.

By RICHARD G. MOULTON, A. M.,

Of Cambridge University, England.

I am requested to furnish information with reference to the University Extension Movement in England. It will be desirable that side by side with the facts I should put the ideas of the movement, for, in matters like these, the ideas are the inspiration of the work; the ideas, moreover, are the same for all, whereas the detailed methods must vary with different localities. The idea of the movement is its soul; the practical working is no more than the body. But body and soul alike are subject to growth, and so it has been in the present case. The English University Extension Movement was in no sense a carefully planned scheme, put forward as a feat of institutional symmetry; it was the product of a simple purpose pursued through many years, amid varying external conditions, in which each modification was suggested by circumstances and tested by experience. And with the complexity of our operations our animating ideas have been striking deeper and growing bolder. Speaking then up to date, I would define the root idea of 'University Extension' in the following simple formula: University Education for the Whole Nation organized on a basis of Itinerant Teachers.

But every clause in this defining formula will need explanation and defence.

The term 'University' Extension has no doubt grown up from the circumstance that the movement in England was started and directed by the universities, which have controlled its operations by precisely the same machinery by which they manage every other department of university business. I do not know that this is an essential feature of the movement. The London branch

1

presents an example of a flourishing organization directed by a committee formed for the purpose, though this committee at present acts in concert with three universities. I can conceive the new type of education managed apart from any university superintendence; only I should look upon such severance as a far more serious evil for the universities than for the popular movement.

But I use the term 'university education' for the further purpose of defining the type of instruction offered. It is thus distinguished from school education, being moulded to meet the wants of adults. It is distinguished from the technical training necessary for the higher handicrafts or for the learned professions. It is no doubt to the busy classes that the movement addresses itself, but we make no secret of the fact that our education will not help them in their business, except that, the mind not being built in water-tight compartments, it is impossible to stimulate one set of faculties without the stimulus reacting upon all the rest. The education that is properly associated with universities is not to be regarded as leading up to anything beyond, but is an end in itself, and applies to life as a whole. And the foundation for university extension is a change, subtle but clear, that may be seen to be coming over the attitude of the public mind to higher education, varying in intensity in different localities, but capable of being encouraged where it is least perceptible,—a change by which education is ceasing to be regarded as a thing proper to particular classes of society or particular periods of life, and is coming to be recognized as one of the permanent interests of life, side by side with such universal interests as religion and politics. For persons of leisure and means such growing demand can be met by increased activity of the universities; University Extension is to be the university of the busy.

My definition puts the hope of extending university education in this sense to the whole nation without exception. I am aware that to some minds such indiscriminate extension will seem like an educational communism, on a par with benevolent schemes for redistributing the wealth of society so as to give everybody a comfortable income all round. But it surely ought not to be necessary to explain that in proposing a universal system of education we are not meaning that what each individual draws from the system will be the same in all cases. In this as in every other public benefit that which each person draws from it must depend upon that which he brings to it. University Extension may be conceived as a stream flowing from the high ground of universities through the length and breadth of the country; from this stream each individual helps himself according to his means and his needs; one takes but a cupful, another uses a bucket, a third claims to have a cistern to himself: every one suits his own capacity, while our duty is to see that the stream is pure and that it is kept running.

The truth is that the wide-reaching purpose of University Extension will seem visionary or practicable according to the conception formed of education, as to what in education is essential and what accidental. If I am asked whether I think of shop-assistants, porters, factory-hands, miners, dock or agricultural laborers, women with families and constant home duties, as classes of people who can be turned into economists, physicists, literary critics, art connoisseurs,—I admit that I have no such idea. But I do believe, or rather, from my experience in England I know, that all such classes can be *interested* in economic, scientific, literary and artistic questions. And I say boldly that to interest in intellectual pursuits is the essential of education, in comparison with which all other educational purposes must be called secondary. I do not consider that a child has been taught to read unless he has been made to like reading; I find it difficult to think of a man as having received a classical education if the man, however scholarly, leaves college with no interest in classical literature such as will lead him to go on reading for himself. In education the interest is the life. If a system of instruction gives discipline, method, and even originating power, without rousing a lasting love for the subject studied, the whole process is but a mental galvanism, generating a delusive activity that ceases when the connection between instructor and pupil is broken off. But if a teacher makes it his first business to stir up an interest in the matter of study, the education becomes self-continuing when teacher and pupil have parted, and the subject becomes its own educator. If then it be conceded that the essence of education is to interest, does it not seem a soberly practical purpose that we should open up to the whole nation without exception an interest in intellectual pursuits?

I take my stand on the broad moral ground that every human being, from the highest to the lowest, has two sides to his life—his work and his leisure. To be without work in life is selfishness and sloth. But if a man or woman is so entangled in routine duties as never to command leisure, we have a right to say to such persons that they are leading an immoral life. Such an individual has no claim to the title of a working man, he is a slave. It may be cruel circumstances that have thus absorbed him in business, but that does not alter the fact: slavery was a misfortune rather than a fault to those who suffered it, but in any case to be content with slavery is a crime. Once get society to recognize the duty of leisure, and there is immediately a scope for such institutions as University Extension that exist for the purpose of giving intellectual interests for such leisure time. The movement is thus one of the greatest movements for the ' raising of the masses.' With a large section of the people there is, at the present moment, no conception of ' rising ' in life, except that of rising out of one social rank into another. This last is of course a perfectly legitimate ambition, but it is outside the present discussion: University Extension knows nothing of social distinctions. It has to do with a far more important mode of ' rising ' in life,—that of rising in the rank to which a man happens to belong at the moment, whether it be the rank in which he started or any other. There is a saying that all men are equal after dinner: and it is true that, while in the material wealth we seek in our working hours equality is a chimera, yet in the intellectual pursuits that belong to leisure there is no bar to the equality of all, except the difference of individual capacity and desire. Macaulay tells of the Dutch farmers who worked in the fields all day, and at night read the Georgics in the original. Scotch and American universities are largely attended by students who have had to engage in menial duties all the summer in order to gain funds for their high education during the winter. And every University Extension lecturer, highly trained specialist as he is, will testify how his work has continually brought him

into contact with persons of the humblest social condition whom a
moment's conversation has made him recognize as his intellectual
equals. No one has any difficulty in understanding that in religious intercourse and experience all classes stand upon an equality ;
and I have spoken of the foundation for the University Extension
movement as being the growing recognition of education as a permanent human interest akin to religion. The experience of a
few years has sufficiently demonstrated the possibility of arousing
such interest: to make it universal is no more than a practical
question of time, money and methods.

But no doubt when we come to *modus operandi* the main difficulty of the movement is the diversity of the classes it seeks to
approach—diversity in individual capacity, in leisure, means, and
previous training. Opposite policies have been urged upon us.
Some have said : Whatever you do, you must never lower the
standard ; let the Extension movement present outside the universities precisely the same education as the universities themselves
are giving, however long you may have to wait for its acceptance.
On the other hand, it has been urged : You must go first where
you are most needed ; be content with a makeshift education until
the people are ready for something better. The movement has
accepted neither of these policies, but has made a distinction
between two elements of university training—method and curriculum. So far as method is concerned we have considered that we
are bound to be not less thorough, but more thorough, if possible,
than the universities themselves, in proportion as our clients work
under peculiar difficulties. But in the matter of curriculum we
have felt it our first duty to be elastic, and to offer little or much
as may in each case be desired. Accordingly, we have elaborated
an educational unit—the three months' course of instruction in a
single subject : this unit course we have used all the resources we
could command for making as thorough in method as possible ;
where more than this is desired, we arrange that more in a combination or series of such unit courses. The instruction can thus
be taken by retail or wholesale: but in all cases it must be admin-
istered on the same rigorous method.

The key to the whole system is thus the unit course of three
months' instruction in a single subject. The method of such a

course is conveyed by the technical terms lecture, syllabus, exercises, class. The lectures are addressed to audiences as miscellaneous as the congregation of a church, or the people in a street car; and it is the duty of the teacher to attract such miscellaneous audiences, as well as to hold and instruct them. Those who do nothing more than simply attend the lectures will at least have gained the education of continuous interest; it is something to have one's attention kept upon the same subject for three months together. But it may be assumed that in every such audience there will be a nucleus of students, by which term we simply mean persons willing to do some work between one lecture and another. The lectures are delivered no oftener than once a week; for the idea is not that the lectures convey the actual instruction —great part of which is better obtained from books, but the office of the lecture is to throw into prominence the salient points of the study, and rouse the hearers to read for themselves. The course of instruction is laid down in the syllabus—a document of perhaps thirty or forty pages, sold for a trifling sum; by referring for details to the pages of books this pamphlet can be made to serve as a text-book for the whole course, making the teacher independent in his order of exposition of any other text-book. The syllabus assists the general audience in following the lectures without the distraction of taking notes; and guides the reading and thinking of the students during the week. The syllabus contains a set of 'exercises' on each lecture. These exercises, unlike examination questions or 'quizzes,' are not tests of memory, but are intended to train the student to work for himself; they are thus to be done under the freest conditions—at home, with full leisure, and all possible access to books, notes or help from other persons. The written answers are sent to the lecturer for marginal comment, and returned by him at the 'class.' This class is a second meeting for students and others, at which no formal lecture is given, but there is free talk on points suggested to the teacher by the exercises he has received: the usual experience is that it is more interesting than the lecture. This weekly routine of lecture, syllabus-reading, exercise and class goes on for a period of twelve weeks. There is then an 'examination' in the work of the course held for students who desire to take it. Certificates are given by the

university, but it is an important arrangement that these certificates
are awarded *jointly* on the result of the weekly exercises and the
final examination.

The subjects treated have been determined by the demand.
Literature stands at the head in popularity, history with economy
is but little behind. All the physical sciences have been freely
asked for. Art constitutes a department of work ; but it is art-
appreciation, not art-production ; the movement has no function
to train artists, but to make audiences and visitors to art-galleries
more intelligent. It will be observed that the great study known
as ' Classics ' is not mentioned in this list. But it is an instruc-
tive fact that a considerable number of the courses in literature
have been on subjects of Greek and Latin literature treated in
English, and some of these have been at once the most successful
in numbers and the most technical in treatment. I am not without hope that our English University Extension may react upon
our English universities, and correct the vicious conception of
classical studies which gives to the great mass of university men
a more or less scholarly hold upon ancient languages without
any interest whatever in ancient literatures.

This university extension method claims to be an advance on
existing systems partly because under no circumstances does it
ever give lectures unaccompanied by a regular plan of reading
and exercises for students. These exercises moreover are designed,
not for mental drill, but for stimulus to original work. The association of students with a general audience is a gain to both
parties. Many persons follow regularly the instruction of the
class who have not participated in the exercises. Moreover, the
students, by their connection with the popular audience, are saved
from the academic bias which is the besetting sin of teachers :
more human interest is drawn into the study. The same effect
follows from the miscellaneous character of the students who
contribute exercises. High university graduates, experts in
special pursuits, deeply cultured individuals who have never
before had any field in which to exhibit the fruits of their culture,
as well as persons whose spelling and writing would pass muster
nowhere else, or casual visitors from the world of business, or
young men and women fresh from school, or even children

writing in round text,—all these classes may be represented in a single week's work; and the papers sent in will vary in elaborateness from a scrawl on a post-card to a magazine article or treatise. I have received an exercise of such a character that the student considerately furnished me with an index; I remember one longer still, but as this hailed from a lunatic asylum I will quote it only for illustrating the diversity of the spheres reached by the movement. Study participated in by such diverse classes cannot but have an all-roundness which is to teachers and students one of the main attractions of the movement.

But we shall be expected to judge our system by results: and, so far as the unit courses are concerned, we have every reason to be satisfied. Very few persons fail in our final examinations, and yet examiners report that the standard in university extension is substantially the same as that in the universities—our pass students being on a par with pass men in the universities, our students of 'distinction' reaching the standard of honors schools. Personally I attach high importance to results which can never be expressed in statistics. We are in a position to assert that a successful course perceptibly influences the *tone* of a locality for the period it lasts: librarians volunteer reports of an entirely changed demand for books, and we have even assurances that the character of conversation at 'five o'clock teas' has undergone marked alteration. I may be permitted an anecdote illustrating the impression made upon the universities themselves. I once heard a brilliant university lecturer, who had had occasional experience of extension teaching, describe a course of investigation which had interested him. With an eye to business I asked him if he would not give it in an extension course. He became grave. "Well, no," he replied, "I have not thought it out sufficiently for that;" and when he saw my look of surprise he added, "You know, anything goes down in college; but when I have to face your mature classes I must know my ground well." I believe the impression thus suggested is not uncommon amongst experts who really know the movement.

Our results are much less satisfactory when we turn to the other side of our system, and enquire as to curriculum. It must be admitted that the larger part of our local centres can only

take unit courses; there may be often a considerable interval
between one course and another; or where courses are taken
regularly the necessity of meeting popular interest involves a
distracting variety of subjects; while an appreciable portion of
our energies have to be taken up with preliminary half-courses,
rather intended to illustrate the working of the movement than
as possessing any high educational value. The most important
advance from the unit course is the Affiliation system of Cambridge university. By this a town that becomes regularly affiliated, has arranged for it a series of unit courses, put together
upon proper sequence of educational topics, and covering some
three or four years: students satisfying the lecturers and examiners in this extended course are recognized as 'Students affiliated' (S. A.), and can at any time enter the university with the
status of second year's men,—the local work being accepted in
place of one year's residence and study. Apart from this, the
steps in our educational ladder other than the first are still in the
stage of prophecy. But it is universally recognized that this
drawback is a matter solely of funds: once let the movement
command endowment and the localities will certainly demand the
wider curriculum that the universities are only too anxious to
supply.

The third point in our definition was that the movement was
to be organized on a basis of itinerant teachers. This differenti-
ates University Extension from local colleges, from correspondence teaching, and from the systems of which Chautauqua is the
type. The chief function of a university is to teach, and University Extension must stand or fall with its teachers. It may
or may not be desirable on other grounds to multiply universities;
but there is no necessity for it on grounds of popular education,
the itinerancy being a sufficient means of bringing any university
into touch with the people as a whole. And the adoption of such
a system seems to be a natural step in the evolution of universities.
In the middle ages the whole body of those who sought a liberal
education were to be found crowded into the limits of university
towns, where alone were teachers to listen to and manuscripts to
copy: the population of such university centres then numbered
hundreds where to-day it numbers tens. The first university

extension was the invention of printing, which sent the books itinerating through the country, and reduced to a fraction the actual attendance at the university, while it vastly increased the circle of the educated. The time has now come to send teachers to follow the books: the ideas of the university being circulated through the country as a whole, while residence at a university is reserved as the apex only of the university system.

An itinerancy implies central and local management, and travelling lecturers who connect the two. The central management is a university, or its equivalent; this is responsible for the educational side of the movement, and negotiates for the supply of its courses of instruction at a fixed price per course.[1] The local management may be in the hands of a committee formed for the purpose, or of some local institution—such as a scientific or literary club or institute—which may care to connect itself with the universities. On the local management devolves the raising funds for the university fee, and for local expenses, as well as the duty of putting the advantages of the course offered before the local community. The widest diversity of practice prevails in reference to modes of raising funds. A considerable part of the cost will be met by the tickets of those attending the lectures, the prices of which I have known to vary from a shilling to a guinea for the unit course, while admission to single lectures has varied from a penny to half a crown. But all experience goes to show that only a part of this cost can be met in this way; individual courses may bring in a handsome profit, but taking account over various terms and various districts, we find that not more than two-thirds of the total cost will be covered by ticket money. And even this is estimated on the assumption that no more than the unit course is aimed at: while even for this the choice of subjects, and the chance of continuity of subject from term to term are seriously limited by the consideration of meeting cost as far as possible from fees. University Extension is a system of higher education, and higher education has no market value, but needs the help of endowment. But the present age is no way behind past ages in the number of

---

[1] The Cambridge fee is £45 per course of three months.

generous citizens it exhibits as ready to help good causes. The millionaire who will take up University Extension will leave a greater mark on the history of his country than even the pious founder of university scholarships and chairs. And even if individuals fail us, we have the common purse of the public or the nation to fall back upon.

The itinerant lecturers, not less than the university and the local management, have responsibility for the progress of the cause. An extension lecturer must be something more than a good teacher, something more even than an attractive lecturer: he must be imbued with the ideas of the movement, and ever on the watch for opportunities of putting them forward. It is only the lecturer who can maintain in audiences the feeling that they are not simply receiving entertainment or instruction which they have paid for, but that they are taking part in a public work, and are responsible for giving their locality a worthy place in a national scheme of university education. The lecturer again must mediate between the local and the central management, always ready to assist local committees with suggestions from the experience of other places, and equally attentive to bringing the special wants of different centres before the university authorities. The movement is essentially a teaching movement, and it is to the body of teachers I look for the discovery of the further steps in the development of popular education. For such a purpose lecturers and directors alike must be imbued with the missionary spirit. For University Extension is a missionary university, not content with supplying culture, but seeking to stimulate the demand for it. This is just the point in which education in the past has shown badly in comparison with religion or politics. When a man is touched with religious ideas he seeks to make converts, when he has views on political questions he agitates to make his views prevail: culture on the other hand has been only too often cherished as a badge of exclusiveness, instead of the very consciousness of superior education being felt as a responsibility which could only be satisfied by efforts to educate others. To infuse a missionary spirit into culture is not the least purpose of University Extension.

I cannot resist the temptation to carry forward this thought from the present into the future. In University Extension so

described may we not see a germ for the University of the Future?
I have made the foundation of our movement the growing conception of education as a permanent interest of adult life side
by side with religion and politics. The change is at best only
beginning; it tasks the imagination to conceive all it will imply
when it is complete. To me it appears that this expanding view
of education is the third of the three great waves of change the
succession of which has made up our modern history. There was
a time when religion itself was identified with a particular class,
the clergy alone thinking out what the rest of the nation simply
accepted; then came the series of revolutions popularly summed
up as the Reformation, by which the whole adult nation claimed
to think for itself in matters of religion, and the special profession of the clergy became no more than a single element in the
religious life of the nation. Again, there has been in the past a
distinct governing class, to which the rest of society submitted;
until a series of political revolutions lifted the whole adult population into self-government, using the services of political experts,
but making public progress the interest of all. Before the more
quiet changes of the present age the conception of an isolated
learned class is giving way before the ideal of a national culture,
in which universities will still be centres for educational experts,
while University Extension offers liberal education to all, until
educationally the whole adult population will be just as much
within the university as politically the adult population is within
the constitution. It would appear then that the university of
such a future would be by no means a repetition of existing types,
such as Oxford or Cambridge, Harvard or Johns Hopkins.
These institutions would exist and be more flourishing than ever,
but they would all be merged in a wider ' University of England,'
or ' University of America'; and, just as the state means the
whole nation acting in its political capacity through municipal
or national institutions, so the university would mean the whole
adult nation acting in its educational capacity through whatever
institutions might be found desirable. Such a university would
never be chartered; no building could ever house it; no royal
personage or president of the United States would ever be asked
to inaugurate it; the very attempt to found it would imply mis-

conception of its essential character. It would be no more than
a floating aggregation of voluntary associations; like the companies of which a nation's commerce is made up such associations
would not be organized, but would simply tend to coöperate
because of their common object. Each association would have
its local and its central side, formed for the purpose of mediating
between the wants of a locality and the educational supply offered
by universities or similar central institutions. No doubt such a
scheme is widely different from the ideal education of European
countries, so highly organized from above that the minister of
education can look at his watch and know at any moment all
that is being done throughout the country. On the contrary the
genius of the Anglo-Saxon race leans towards self-help; it has
been the mission of the race in the past to develop self-government in religion and politics, it remains to crown this work with
the application of the voluntary system to liberal education.

In indulging this piece of speculation I have had a practical
purpose before me. If what I have described be a reasonable
forecast for the University of the Future, does it not follow that
University Extension, as the germ of it, presents a field for the
very highest academic ambition? To my mind it appears that
existing types of university have reached a point where further
development in the same direction would mean decline. In
English universities the ideal is 'scholarship.' Scholarship is a
good thing, and we produce it. But the system which turns
out a few good scholars every year passes over the heads of the
great mass of university students without having awakened
them to any intellectual life; the universities are scholarship-
factories producing good articles but with a terrible waste of raw
material. The other main type of university enthrones 'research'
as its summum bonum. Possibly research is as good a purpose as
a man can set before him, but it is not the sole aim in life. And
when one contemplates the band of recruits added each year to
the army of investigators, and the choice of ever minuter fields—
not to say lanes and alleys—of research, one is led to doubt
whether research is not one of the disintegrating forces of society,
and whether ever increasing specialisation must not mean a perpetual narrowing of human sympathies in the intellectual leaders

of mankind. Both types of university appear to me to present the phenomena of a country suffering from the effects of over-production, where the energies of workers had been concentrated upon adding to the sum of wealth, and all too little attention had been given to the distribution of that wealth through the different ranks of the community. Just at this point the University Extension movement appears to recall academic energy from production to distribution; suggesting that devotion to physics, economics, art, can be just as truly shown by raising new classes of the people to an interest in physical and economic and æsthetic pursuits, as by adding to the discoveries of science, or increasing the mass of art products. To the young graduate, conscious that he has fairly mastered the teaching of the past, and that he has within him powers to make advances, I would suggest the question whether, even for the highest powers, there is any worthier field than to work through University Extension towards the University of the Future.